SATURDAY & SUNDAYS

SEASONAL WEEKEND MENUS

Written and styled by Kay Francis

Photography by Gerry Colley

NEW
HOLLAND

First published in Australia in 2000 by
New Holland Publishers (Australia) Pty Ltd
Sydney • Auckland • London • Cape Town

14 Aquatic Drive Frenchs Forest NSW 2086 Australia
218 Lake Road Northcote Auckland New Zealand
24 Nutford Place London W1H 6DQ United Kingdom
80 McKenzie Street Cape Town 8001 South Africa

National Library of Australia Cataloguing-in-Publication Data:
Francis, Kay, 1952–
Saturdays Sundays—seasonal weekend menus.
Includes index.
ISBN 1 86436 591 9
1. Cookery. I. Colley, Gerry, 1959–. II. Title.
641

Publishing General Manager: Jane Hazell
Publisher: Averill Chase
Senior Editor: Monica Ban
Copy Editor: Lynn Cole
Designer: Peta Nugent
Photographer's Assistant: Alison Pirlo
Reproduction: Colour Symphony
Printer: South China Printing

Photographic credit: Lemons on page 132 by Philip White
Acknowledgements: Cover photograph ceramics from Mud Australia

For Celia, who loves weekends

PREFACE

This book is as much about time as it is about food and cooking. Weekend time has a unique personality. It is cheese to the chalk of weekday, workday time. The smells are different, the sounds and movements have a different rhythm, the pace is of our choosing. We wear different clothes and eat different food.

You choose the pattern of your two-day break. One dilemma is that there are so many options and, being weak in the face of temptation, we want them all. Cramming our weekends often means superficial exposure to many things and, over a period, satisfaction is consumed by rush. We face the new work week exhausted, suffering from the Monday blues.

Try a change of pace, share time with friends, make conversation that nurtures and have some real relaxation. Cooking for people you choose to be with doesn't necessarily mean stress and an expensive dinner party. Tune into the season, your needs, their needs. Grab spontaneity as it flits by. Get together for breakfast and fill your house with the scent of quinces, baked all night long. Eat ice-cream at midnight, or drag a Persian rug onto the grass and eat peaches under a full moon. Involve your children and spend time eating with them, without setting yourself up for frustration. Eat outdoors or make a picnic. Enjoy the process—it's fun, not 'trouble'.

The menus in this book are suggestions, planned for the seasons. Mix them up to suit your life. Change them, improvise on their themes and make them your own. All the ingredients should be readily available, but use the freshest you can get. Plant some herbs. If your local market doesn't stock something you want, ask for it. Chances are other people are asking for it, too.

Many of the recipes are gluten-free. Where flour is used in pastry, you can substitute gluten-free flour. Just add an egg yolk to the mixture to provide some of the missing binding agent. Once again, feel free to experiment.

Most of all, relax and enjoy yourself.

Kay Frances

SPRING

SUMMER

AUTUMN

WINTER

SPRING

BREAKFAST TO CELEBRATE THE SEASON

| SERVES SIX

FRUIT PLATTER WITH VANILLA-SEED JUNKET

FRUIT: *3 ruby grapefruit, segmented, 150g (5oz) blueberries, 250g (8oz) cape gooseberries, halved, 1 mango, peeled and sliced, 3 star fruit, sliced, 2 nashi pears, sliced*
- *2 stalks lemongrass, roughly chopped*
- *1 cup (220g/7oz) raw sugar*

VANILLA-SEED JUNKET: *3 junket tablets*
- *3 cups (750ml/24fl oz) milk*
- *Rind of 1 lemon, julienned finely*
- *Seeds from 1 1/2 vanilla pods*

To make junket, crush junket tablets and dissolve in 2–3 tablespoons cold water. Combine milk, rind and vanilla seeds in a saucepan. Heat to barely warm, then quickly stir in junket. Immediately pour into 6 glasses or bowls, each about 1/2 cup (125ml/4fl oz). Stand still for 15 minutes. Refrigerate. Combine fruit and chill. Simmer lemongrass, sugar and 1 cup (250ml/8fl oz) water. Bring to the boil, stirring to dissolve sugar, and simmer for 5 minutes. Cool. Strain over fruit. Serve each junket in its glass, with fruit.

...

TOASTED WALNUT BREAD WITH CREAMY SCRAMBLED EGG IN A SPINACH NEST

- *60g (2oz) butter*
- *1 teaspoon freshly grated nutmeg*
- *1 bunch English spinach, washed*
- *12 eggs*
- *1 cup (250ml/8fl oz) pouring cream*
- *1 loaf walnut bread, sliced and toasted*
- *Cream cheese or quark, for spreading*

Melt half the butter in a saucepan and add nutmeg and spinach. Cover and cook over low heat for 15 minutes, shaking pan occasionally. Whisk eggs with cream and season with salt and cracked black pepper. Melt remaining butter in a frying pan over medium heat. Pour in egg. Stir gently as mixture cooks; remove from heat while lumpy and still slightly creamy. (It will continue to cook.) Overcooking will cause egg to become watery. Cut toast into fingers or triangles. Spread with cream cheese or quark. Serve scrambled egg in a nest of toast fingers and spinach.

...

DRUNKEN MANDARIN GEMS

- *1 Honey Murcott mandarin, about 200g (6 1/2oz), cut into 2cm dice, seeds discarded*
- *1 2/3 cups (200g/6 1/2oz) almond meal*
- *1 teaspoon baking powder*
- *1/2 cup (110g/3 1/2oz) caster sugar*
- *2 eggs*

SYRUP: *1/4 cup (60g/2oz) caster sugar*
- *1/3 cup (80ml/2 1/2 fl oz) Grand Marnier or Cointreau*

Preheat oven to 180°C/350°F/Gas Mark 4. Lightly spray 3 trays of 12 tiny muffin cups with oil. Combine ingredients in a blender or food processor and blend until fairly smooth. Fill each cup with the mixture, so it is level with the top edge. Bake for 10 minutes. Cool slightly; turn out into a shallow tray. Meanwhile, boil sugar and 1/4 cup (60ml/2fl oz) water for 8 minutes, or until syrup is just beginning to colour. Remove from heat and stir in alcohol. Pour over warm gems. Best eaten within 2 days.
Makes 36 bite-size gems.

Opposite: Fruit platter with Vanilla-Seed Junket.

SOMETHING SUBSTANTIAL FOR BRUNCH

SERVES SIX

GRILLED CHICKEN AND DUCK SAUSAGES ON POTATO FRITTERS

- *4 large potatoes*
- *Juice of 1 lemon*
- *500g (1lb) butternut pumpkin*
- *200g (6½oz) quark, at room temperature*
- *3 eggs, beaten lightly*
- *3 tablespoons flour*
- *1 teaspoon freshly grated nutmeg*
- *About ⅓ cup (30g/1oz) grated parmesan*
- *60g (2oz) butter*
- *6 duck sausages*
- *6 chicken, pinenut and spinach sausages*
- *Fresh herb of your choice, for garnish*

Heat oven to lowest setting to warm plates. Peel potatoes and grate into a colander. Rinse under cold water and toss with lemon juice. Remove seeds from pumpkin and steam flesh (skin on) until tender. Scrape flesh from skin and mash with quark; season to taste with salt and freshly ground black pepper. Keep warm.

Combine egg, flour, nutmeg and parmesan with potato. Season to taste. Melt butter in a heavy-based frying pan and cook large spoonfuls of potato over medium–high heat until crisp and golden on both sides. Keep warm.

Meanwhile, cook sausages in a grill pan until almost done. Cut each thick sausage in half lengthways and grill the cut sides until crisp. To serve, pile mashed pumpkin onto potato fritters and stack sausage fingers around. Garnish with herbs.

STICKY HEART TARTS

- *12 slices brioche, cut 6mm (¼in) thick*
- *45g (1½oz) butter, melted*
- *250g (8oz) strawberries, chopped*
- *¼ cup (50g/2oz) brown sugar*
- *1 teaspoon cassis*
- *Icing sugar, to serve*

Preheat oven to 200°C/400°F/Gas Mark 5. Brush 12 individual heart-shaped tart tins, each about 7.5cm (3in), or small muffin tins, with butter. Cut heart shapes or circles, slightly larger than the tins, from brioche slices. (Process any scraps into crumbs and freeze.) Press into tins and brush with butter. Combine strawberries, brown sugar and cassis and spoon into brioche cases. Bake for 10 minutes, reduce temperature to 180°C/350°F/Gas Mark 4 and bake for 10 minutes more, or until brioche is crisp. Cool in tins. Dust with icing sugar and serve at room temperature.

SUBSTITUTES

Substitute framboise, Cointreau, amaretto or orange juice for cassis, if desired.
Quark is a fresh, soft white cheese, available in tubs from the cheese counter of your deli.
Creamed cottage cheese is a good substitute.
Ready-rolled puff pastry can be used for bases of sticky heart tarts.

Opposite: Grilled Chicken and Duck Sausages on Potato Fritters.

Morning COFFEE AND THE WORKS

| Serves eight

Little Apple Tarts

PASTRY: *1 cup (150g/5oz) plain flour*
• *³/4 cup (100g/3 ¹/2oz) ground almonds or macadamias*
• *Finely grated rind of 1 lemon*
• *125g (4oz) unsalted butter*
FILLING: *1 large Firm Gold or Golden Delicious apple*
• *45g (1 ¹/2oz) unsalted butter, melted*
• *2 tablespoons honey*
• *Squeeze of lemon juice*
• *Icing sugar, to serve*

To make pastry, combine flour, ground nuts and rind and rub in butter until mixture resembles coarse breadcrumbs. Knead with your hand until mixture clings together. Shape into a disc, wrap in plastic wrap (film) and refrigerate for 20 minutes.

Preheat oven to 190°C/375°F/Gas Mark 4. Lightly grease 12 shallow patty tins, each about 6cm (2¹/2in) in diameter. Halve and core apples and slice thinly. Combine with melted butter and

Opposite: Coconut Tarts and Little Apple Tarts.

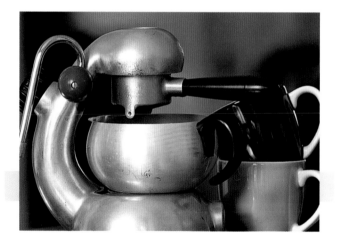

1 tablespoon honey, to coat apples all over. Roll out pastry thinly. Using a fluted cookie cutter, cut out 12 circles to fit prepared patty tins. Arrange apple slices in cases and bake for 20 minutes, or until pastry is golden and apples are soft. Warm remaining honey with lemon juice. Brush on tarts and return to oven for 2 minutes. Cool for 15 minutes in tins, loosen tarts and cool completely. Dust with icing sugar to serve. Tarts are best eaten within 24 hours.
Makes 12.

DENSE COFFEE NUT CAKE

- *1 tablespoon instant espresso coffee*
- *1 tablespoon dark rum*
- *185g (6oz) dark chocolate, broken into small pieces*
- *125g (4oz) unsalted butter, at room temperature*
- *½ cup (110g/3½oz) raw sugar*
- *5 eggs, separated*
- *1⅔ cups (200g/6½oz) almond meal*
- *500g (1lb) mixed nuts (brazils, hazelnuts and macadamias), chopped fairly finely*
- *Icing sugar, for dusting*

Preheat oven to 180°C/350°F/Gas Mark 4.
Grease a 16cm (6½in) square cake tin
and line base with baking paper.
Dissolve coffee in 2 tablespoons water. Add rum.
Melt chocolate in a bowl over simmering water or
in a microwave oven. Cool slightly while preparing
remaining ingredients. Stir in coffee mixture.
Beat butter and sugar until light and fluffy.
Beat in chocolate and rum mixture. Add egg yolks,
one at a time, beating well after each addition.
Stir in almond meal and chopped nuts.
Whisk egg whites until soft peaks form and
fold into cake mixture until just combined.
Pour into prepared tin and bake for 45–50 minutes,
or until cake is pulling away from edges of tin
(the centre will be fairly soft). Cool for 10 minutes
in tin, loosen edges with a metal spatula and invert
cake onto a wire rack. Leave tin in place and cool
completely; remove tin. Place cake on a serving plate,
cover and refrigerate for at least 2 hours. Dust
with icing sugar and cut into small slices
(use a sharp finely serrated knife).

CUTTING AND STORING

This cake cuts more neatly if the nuts are chopped
fairly fine. The cake keeps well, refrigerated,
for several days.

COCONUT TARTS

PASTRY: *1½ cups (225g/7oz) plain flour*
- *1 cup (90g/3oz) desiccated coconut*
- *125g (4oz) unsalted butter*
- *Finely grated rind of ½ lemon*
- *1 tablespoon lemon juice*
- *2 egg yolks*

FILLING: *1 cup (75g/2½oz) shredded coconut*
- *1 tablespoon plain flour*
- *½ cup (125ml/4fl oz) light corn syrup*
- *2 egg whites, whisked to soft peaks*

To make pastry, combine flour and coconut and rub
in butter until mixture resembles coarse breadcrumbs.
Stir in rind and combined lemon juice and yolks.
Knead with your hand until mixture clings together.
Shape into a disc, wrap in plastic wrap (film)
and refrigerate for 20 minutes.
For filling, soak coconut in 1 cup (250ml/8fl oz) hot
water for 10 minutes. Drain, pressing out excess water.
Combine with flour and corn syrup. Fold in beaten
whites. Preheat oven to 190°C/375°F/Gas Mark 4.
Lightly grease 8–10 rectangular tart tins,
each about 8cm (3in) long.
Roll out pastry thinly, line tins. (Press any scraps into
a ball, wrap and freeze for another use.) Spoon filling
into tart cases and bake for 15–20 minutes, or until
pastry is golden and filling is puffed and lightly
coloured. Cool in tins.
Makes 8–10.

SUNDAY LUNCH
ON THE PATIO

| SERVES SIX

SMOKED TROUT
ON STEAMED NEW POTATOES
WITH CAPER CREAM

- *12 small new potatoes (chats), steamed in skins, cooled*
- *1 smoked trout*
- *1 cup (250ml/8fl oz) sour cream*
- *2 tablespoons tiny capers*
- *Caper berries, to serve*

Slice each potato into 3 pieces. Place in a single
layer on a serving platter. Remove skin from
trout and lift each fillet from the bones.
Combine cream and capers and drop a teaspoonful
on each potato slice. Top with a piece of trout and
sprinkle with freshly ground black pepper. Place
a small dish of caper berries on the platter to serve.

CAPER BERRIES

Caper berries are the berries of the caper bush; capers
are the flower buds of the same bush. The flavour
is similar and berries and buds are interchangeable.

POACHED PORK WITH LEEK RIBBONS, EGG AND ANCHOVY DRESSING

- *12 cups (3L/96fl oz) chicken stock or mixed stock and water*
- *2 large leeks, tough green tops discarded and remainder cut into thin ribbons*
- *3 bulbs fresh garlic, stalks trimmed and bulbs halved lengthways (or use 4 cloves garlic, crushed, or add garlic chives toward the end of cooking time)*
- *1 carrot, chopped*
- *1 teaspoon white peppercorns*
- *1/2 cup fresh oregano sprigs*
- *2kg (4lb) pork leg, skin removed and reserved*
- *Sea salt*
- *6 hard-boiled eggs, to serve*

SAUCE: *3 egg yolks*
- *1 cup (250ml/8fl oz) light olive oil*
- *45g (1 1/2oz) anchovies in oil, drained*
- *Juice of 1/2 lemon*
- *1/2 cup (125ml/4fl oz) reserved poaching liquid*
- *Oregano sprigs, for garnish*

Bring stock to the boil in a large pot. Add leeks, return to the boil and remove leeks immediately with a slotted spoon. Drain in a colander and set aside. Add garlic, carrot, peppercorns and oregano to stock, bring to the boil. Add pork, cover, reduce heat to low and barely simmer for 20 minutes. Turn off heat and cool meat, in the liquid, to room temperature.

Preheat oven to 250°C/525°F/Gas Mark 7. Slice pork skin into strips 6mm (1/4 in) wide. Sprinkle with sea salt and place strips on a rack over an ovenproof dish. Cook for 10 minutes, reduce temperature to 200°C/400°F/Gas Mark 5 and cook for a further 10 minutes, or until crisp and golden.

Cool at room temperature.

To make sauce, whisk egg yolks with 1 tablespoon oil then add remaining oil in a slow, steady stream, whisking constantly. Whisk in anchovies, combined lemon juice and poaching liquid, until sauce is pale and aerated. (This can be done in a blender.)

Opposite: Poached Pork with Leek Ribbons, Egg and Anchovy Dressing.

To serve, slice pork and quarter eggs. Put a pile of leek on each serving plate, add eggs, pork and crackling. Pour sauce over meat so it will soak through to the leek. Garnish with oregano.

. . .

PINEAPPLE AND ALMOND TART

PASTRY: *1 2/3 cups (200g/6 1/2oz) almond meal*
- *2/3 cup (100g/3 1/2oz) plain flour*
- *90g (3oz) unsalted butter, cubed*
- *1 egg yolk*

FILLING:
- *90g (3oz) unsalted butter, melted*
- *1 cup (250ml/8fl oz) dark (caramel) corn syrup*
- *1/2 fresh pineapple, cut into 1cm (1/2in) dice, drained*
- *1 egg*
- *1 egg white*
- *2/3 cup (160ml/5fl oz) sour cream*
- *3/4 cup (60g/2oz) flaked almonds*
- *Icing sugar, to serve*

To make pastry, combine almond meal and flour in a bowl. Rub in butter until mixture resembles fine breadcrumbs, then stir in yolk and add chilled water, 1 teaspoon at a time, until mixture clings together. Shape pastry into a disc, wrap in baking paper and refrigerate for 15 minutes.

Preheat oven to 200°C/400°F/Gas Mark 5.

Roll pastry out on paper to fit a 23cm (9in) square or round flan tin with removable base. Pastry is quite soft so you may need to patch it with your fingers. Prick base with a fork and place tin in freezer for 5 minutes. Line pastry shell with baking paper, fill with dried beans or rice and bake blind for 20 minutes.

Meanwhile, prepare filling. Whisk butter with corn syrup until thick and pale. Stir in pineapple. In another bowl, whisk egg, egg white and sour cream.

Remove tart from oven, reduce oven temperature to 170°C/340°F/Gas Mark 3. Remove beans or rice and paper. Pour pineapple mixture into hot shell and spread sour cream mixture over top. Sprinkle almonds over cream. Return to oven and bake for 40 minutes, or until filling is firm and almonds are golden brown. Cool. Sprinkle with icing sugar and serve warm or at room temperature.

WHEEL OUT THE BARBECUE FOR LUNCH

SERVES EIGHT

ENTRÉE PLATTER

- 2 bunches baby radish, washed and trimmed
- 200g (6¹/₂oz) neufchatel cheese, cut into cubes
- 1 stick rye bread, sliced
- Small dish of sea salt

Arrange ingredients on a serving platter,
with a spreader knife for the cheese and a small
dish for the radish tops.

...

CAESAR SALAD

- 2 baby cos (romaine) lettuce
- 6 eggs
- 8 rashers bacon, rinds removed
- 60g (2oz) butter
- 3 cloves garlic, crushed
- 1 x 45g (1¹/₂oz) can anchovies, in oil
- 8 thick slices bread, cut into 6mm (¹/₂in) dice
- ³/₄ cup (60g/2oz) flaked parmesan

Opposite: Entrée Platter.

DRESSING: *1 egg*
- 1 clove garlic, crushed
- 1 teaspoon Dijon mustard
- ¹/₃ cup (30g/1oz grated parmesan)
- 1 x 45g (1¹/₂oz) can anchovies, in oil
- ³/₄ cup (190ml/6fl oz) olive oil

Wash and drain lettuce, discarding any tough outer
leaves. Soft-boil eggs (3 minutes). Place in cold water
to halt cooking and cool. Chop bacon into small
cubes, fry in a non-stick pan (or a lightly greased
normal pan) until crisp, stirring frequently. Remove
with a slotted spoon, leaving bacon fat in pan.
Add butter and garlic to pan and cook for 1 minute.
Add oil drained from anchovies and diced bread.
Stir over medium heat until crisp and golden.
Remove from pan and add to bacon. Cool.
For dressing, place all ingredients in blender and
process until smooth. Arrange lettuce on a serving
platter. Shell and halve eggs and place on lettuce.
Sprinkle bacon and croutons on top, then anchovies.
Just before serving, pour dressing over salad and
sprinkle with flaked parmesan.

BARBECUED BEEF STANDING-RIB ROAST

- *1 beef standing-rib roast, 6 ribs, about 2.5kg (3lb) (stand at room temperature for at least 1 hour before cooking)*
- *Mustard seed oil*

Heat barbecue until coals are glowing red. Rub beef with oil and cover rib ends with foil. Cook roast, fat-side-down first, for 1 hour, turning once. Check barbecue during cooking to make sure heat is sufficient and add more fuel if necessary. Stand roast, covered, to rest for 10 minutes before slicing. *Six ribs gives enough meat for eight people.*

MERINGUES SERVED WITH BLOOD ORANGE CURD

- *¹/₂ cup (125ml/4fl oz) egg whites (4–6 eggs, depending on size)*
- *1 ¹/₄ cups (275g/9oz) caster sugar*
- *1 teaspoon lemon juice*
- *2 teaspoons pure icing sugar*

Heat oven to 120°C/250°F/Gas Mark 1.
Line 2 flat baking trays with baking paper. Combine egg whites, sugar, lemon juice and a pinch of salt in bowl of an electric mixer and whisk on high speed for 15 minutes. The mixture should be stiff, glossy and smooth. Sift icing sugar over mixture and, using a large metal spoon, fold in. Use 2 dessert spoons to shape meringues. Take a spoonful of mixture with 1 spoon and, using the other, push mixture into a mound on prepared tray. Don't try to smooth the surface, simply leave mixture as it is. Space mounds at least 2.5cm (1in) apart. Bake for 1¹/₂ hours, then cool in the oven with the door ajar. The meringues should remain quite white, with barely a hint of colour. When quite cold, store in airtight containers until required. Serve with Blood Orange Curd (recipe follows).

MERINGUES

For the most successful meringues, use an electric mixer to beat the whites and sugar.

BLOOD ORANGE CURD

- *4–6 egg yolks (from meringue recipe)*
- *¹/₂ cup (110g/3¹/₂oz) caster sugar*
- *1–1¹/₄ cups (250–310ml/8–10fl oz) blood orange juice (can use navel or valencia orange juice)*
- *3 whole star anise*

Whisk egg yolks with sugar in the top of a double boiler, or in a bowl placed over a saucepan of simmering water, until pale and aerated. Whisk in juice, add star anise and stir mixture over simmering water for about 10 minutes, or until thickened. Do not boil or mixture will curdle. If this happens, whisk another egg yolk in a clean bowl and slowly whisk curdled mixture into it. Spoon into a serving dish and pass separately with meringues (recipe above). *Makes about 1¹/₂ cups (375ml/12fl oz).*

CHAMPAGNE PICNIC IN THE AFTERNOON

PICNICS

Chill the champagne glasses—bury in an Esky (cool box) of ice for transportation.

MUSCAT BISCUITS

- *1 cup (150g/5oz) plain flour*
- *5 tablespoons (90g/3oz) vanilla sugar*
- *60g (2oz) unsalted butter, at room temperature*
- *⅓ cup (80ml/2½ fl oz) muscat or sweet dessert wine*
- *Icing sugar, for dusting*

Sift flour into a bowl and stir in 4 tablespoons of the sugar and a pinch of salt. Rub in butter until mixture resembles fine breadcrumbs. Make a well in the centre, add muscat and stir until just combined. Stand mixture for 10 minutes, stirring occasionally.

Preheat oven to 190°C/375°F/Gas Mark 4. Lightly grease a flat baking tray. Press biscuit mixture into a ball. Roll out, as thinly as possible, on a lightly floured work surface. Sprinkle remaining sugar over dough. Cut into small shapes and place on prepared tray. Bake for 6 minutes, or until edges are just beginning to brown. Transfer to a wire rack and, while edges are still warm, dust with icing sugar.

Cool completely, then store in an airtight container until required.

Makes about 20
(quantity depends on the size you cut the biscuits).

BITES OF WHITE ASPARAGUS WRAPPED IN PROSCIUTTO WITH CHÈVRE

- *12 spears of white asparagus*
- *24 thin slices prosciutto*
- *100g (3¹/₂oz) chèvre*

Trim tough ends of asparagus. Drop spears into boiling water, return to a simmer for 2 minutes, then remove spears with a slotted spoon. Cool.

Place 2 slices prosciutto side-by-side on a work surface. Spread some chèvre along 1 short end, place an asparagus spear on top and roll up in prosciutto. Repeat until all the asparagus is rolled up. Cut each roll diagonally into three pieces. Arrange on a serving plate and sprinkle with freshly ground black pepper.

Serve at room temperature.

ASPARAGUS

Use crisp spears of fresh white (or purple, or green) asparagus. Snap off stalk ends, they will break at exactly the right place. To cool, place them in a single layer. There is no need to rinse under cold water.

ANGEL FOOD CAKE WITH BERRIES AND THICK CREAM

- *1¹/₃ cups (300g/9¹/₂oz) caster sugar, sifted 3 times*
- *1 cup (150g/5oz) plain flour, sifted 5 times*
- *11 egg whites*
- *1 teaspoon salt*
- *1¹/₂ teaspoons cream of tartar*
- *1 teaspoon vanilla essence*
- *Icing sugar, for dusting*
- *Fresh mulberries (or other berries), to serve*
- *Thick cream, to serve*

Preheat oven to 200°C/400°F/Gas Mark 5. Lightly grease an angel food cake tin, or a 25cm (10in) bundt tin. Mix ¹/₃ cup (75g/2¹/₂oz) of the sugar into sifted flour. Beat egg whites with electric mixer until foamy. Add salt, beat for 1 minute more; add cream of tartar and beat for 3 minutes more. Gradually add remaining sugar, beating continually, until mixture is stiff and glossy. Stir in vanilla, then fold in flour in 4 batches. Do not overmix. Spoon mixture into prepared tin and smooth the top a little.

Bake in centre of oven for 10 minutes. Reduce temperature to 150°C/300°F/Gas Mark 2 and bake for 25–30 minutes more, or until a thin skewer inserted into the cake comes out clean. Remove from oven, invert tin on a wire rack and leave tin in place until cake is cold. You may need to release the sides of the cake with a metal spatula to turn it out. Place on a serving plate, dust with icing sugar and serve with berries and cream passed separately.

Opposite: Angel Food Cake with Berries and Thick Cream.

SAVOURY SNACKS
IN THE AFTERNOON

CHEESE STRAWS

- *125g (4oz) unsalted butter*
- *1 cup (150g/5oz) unbleached plain flour*
- *1 ¼ cups (150g/5oz) grated mature cheddar cheese*
- *1 tablespoon walnut oil*

Rub butter into flour until mixture resembles breadcrumbs. Stir in cheese and oil and season to taste with salt and cracked black pepper. Knead into a ball, flatten into a disc, wrap in plastic wrap (film) and refrigerate for 1 hour. Preheat oven to 200°C/400°F/Gas Mark 5. Line flat baking trays with baking paper. Roll dough out on a lightly floured board to 6mm (¼in) thickness, cut into strips and place well apart on baking trays. Bake for 15 minutes, or until golden. Cool on trays. When cold, store in an airtight container.

...

SPICED NEW POTATOES WITH SWEET CHILLI JELLY AND CRÈME FRAÎCHE

- *1kg (2lb) small new potatoes (chats)*
- *1 tablespoon mustard seed oil*
- *1 tablespoon butter, melted*
- *1 teaspoon sea salt*
- *1 tablespoon ground coriander*
- *1 teaspoon ground cumin*
- *Crème fraîche, to serve*

Preheat oven to 220°C/450°F/Gas Mark 6. Wash potatoes and steam until just tender. Place in an ovenproof dish, add remaining ingredients, except crème fraîche, and move potatoes around to coat well. Bake for 15–20 minutes, or until starting to crisp. Serve hot with crème fraîche and Sweet Chilli Jelly (recipe follows).

SWEET CHILLI JELLY: Soak 2 sheets gelatine in cold water for 10 minutes. Combine ½ cup (125ml/4fl oz) sweet chilli sauce and ¼ cup (60ml/2fl oz) ginger vinegar in a small saucepan. Squeeze water from gelatine, add sheets to chilli sauce mixture and stir over medium heat until dissolved. Pour into a 1-cup (250ml/8fl-oz) mould. Refrigerate until set, then turn out.

...

KANGAROO SAUSAGE ROLLS WITH MUSTARD AND GARLIC PASTE

- *3 sheets ready-rolled butter puff or puff pastry*
- *1 tablespoon roasted garlic paste*
- *4 tablespoons Dijon mustard*
- *6 thin kangaroo sausages (or other long thin sausages), skin removed*
- *2 egg yolks*
- *½ cup (125ml/4fl oz) mayonnaise*

Preheat oven to 200°C/400°F/Gas Mark 5. Line 2 baking trays with baking paper. Spread each sheet with garlic paste combined with half the mustard. Place sausages along 2 opposite edges of each pastry sheet. Cut pastry in half down centre. Roll sausages in pastry, finishing with edges under rolls. Cut each roll into 4 equal pieces and place on baking trays. Whisk egg yolks, a pinch of salt and 1 tablespoon water. Brush mixture on rolls, then press a knife into top of each roll to make diagonal score marks. Bake for 10–15 minutes, or until pastry is golden. Serve with combined mayonnaise and remaining mustard. *Makes 24.*

Opposite: Spiced New Potatoes and Kangaroo Sausage Rolls with Mustard and Garlic Paste.

FIRST OF THE CROP DINNER

BROAD BEANS

When buying broad beans, take into account that you will lose about three-quarters of their weight when you discard the pods. For 1kg (2lb) shelled beans, you need to buy 4kg (8lb). If the beans are large, you may want to remove the tough outer skins as well. Young beans, shelled and peeled, are delicious eaten raw with salt.

Opposite: Baby Broad Bean and Chèvre Tart with Lemon Dressing.

SERVES EIGHT

BABY BROAD BEAN AND CHÈVRE TART WITH LEMON DRESSING

- *1 kg (2lb) shelled broad beans (see Broad Beans)*
- *4 sheets frozen ready-rolled puff pastry*
- *1 tablespoon fennel seeds*
- *4 eggs*
- *300g (9½oz) chèvre*
- *Finely julienned rind and juice of 1 lemon (reserve some rind for garnish)*

LEMON DRESSING:
- *⅓ cup (80ml/2½ fl oz) mustard seed oil*
- *2 tablespoons lemon juice*

Steam beans for 15 minutes, cool until easy to handle and peel off tough outer skins, if desired.

Preheat oven to 220°C/450°F/Gas Mark 6. Lightly grease 8 individual fluted tart tins with removable bases, each 12cm (4¾in) in diameter. Place 2 pastry sheets on a work surface. Sprinkle each with half the fennel seeds. Press 1 of the 2 remaining pastry sheets on top of each. Using a tart tin as a guide, cut 8 circles from the pastry and gently press each into a prepared tin. Place on flat oven trays and refrigerate while preparing filling.

Lightly whisk eggs, stir in beans and crumbled chèvre. Stir in lemon rind and juice. Spoon mixture into pastry cases and bake for 20 minutes, or until pastry is puffed and golden.

Whisk dressing ingredients together and season to taste with salt and freshly ground black pepper. Serve tarts hot with dressing spooned over; garnish with rind.

Slowly Poached Veal Shank with Spring Vegetables

- *2kg (4lb) mixed spring vegetables: baby turnips, carrots, baby zucchini (courgettes), baby leek, new garlic, baby fennel, butter beans, brussels sprouts*
- *8 cups (2L/64fl oz) veal stock*
- *2kg (4lb) sliced veal shank, taken from very young veal, so meat is pale and pieces small*
- *Mixed fresh herbs: chervil, oregano, thyme, bay leaves, parsley, tied in a bunch*
- *1 teaspoon black peppercorns*
- *1 teaspoon mustard seeds*
- *3 tablespoons veal glacé*
- *Fresh herbs, chopped, for garnish*

Prepare vegetables. Trim and peel turnips, trim and scrub carrots, wash zucchini, trim leeks, garlic and beans, quarter brussels sprouts.
Heat stock in a deep ovenproof pot. Drop in root vegetables and cook for 5 minutes. Add remaining vegetables. Bring to a simmer and, using a slotted spoon, transfer vegetables immediately to a bowl. Cover and set aside.
Preheat oven to 150°C/300°F/Gas Mark 2. Have stock simmering on top of stove. Add veal, herbs, peppercorns and mustard seeds. Transfer to oven and cook, covered, for 3 hours.
Using a slotted spoon, remove meat into a serving bowl. Cover with foil and keep warm. Strain stock into another large saucepan through a fine sieve lined with damp muslin. Boil rapidly to reduce by about one-third. Stir in veal glacé and boil for 5 minutes. Add vegetables and heat through; using a slotted spoon transfer to a warmed serving dish. Garnish with herbs. Pour some hot stock over meat and pour remainder into a warmed jug to serve.

VEAL SHANKS AND GLACÉ

Most butchers will order young veal shanks in for you; some keep them on hand, frozen. This recipe does not suit large, dark shanks. Prepared veal glacé is available in small jars from delicatessens and some butchers.

Lemon Crème Brûlée with Sweet Lemons

- *2½ cups (600ml/20fl oz) pouring cream*
- *1 vanilla bean, split lengthways*
- *Rind of 2 lemons, finely julienned*
- *4 egg yolks*
- *¼ cup (60g/2oz) caster sugar*
- *¼ cup (50g/2oz) brown sugar*

SWEET LEMONS: *4 lemons, sliced thinly*
- *1 cup (220g/7oz) caster sugar*
- *1 teaspoon vanilla essence*

Preheat oven to 160°C/325°F/Gas Mark 3.
Heat cream, vanilla bean and lemon rind in top of a double boiler. Whisk yolks with 2 tablespoons of the caster sugar until pale and fluffy. Strain hot cream onto this, stirring. Place bowl over simmering water and cook, stirring, until mixture coats the back of spoon. Do not boil or custard will curdle.
Pour into a shallow 3-cup (750ml/24floz) ovenproof dish and bake for about 8 minutes, or until a skin forms on top. Remove and cool, then refrigerate for 2 hours. Preheat grill to very hot. Sprinkle remaining caster sugar and brown sugar (combined) over top of custard. Place dish under grill, at least 10cm (4in) away from heat, until sugar forms a layer of caramel. Rotate the dish to expose sugar evenly to the heat. Refrigerate. Combine lemon ingredients in a saucepan, stirring until sugar dissolves. Simmer until lemon slices are translucent. Spoon into a bowl and refrigerate.

TANGY FLAVOURS FOR DINNER

SERVES SIX

STUFFED BABY EGGPLANT

- *250g (8oz) minced chicken*
- *250g (8oz) minced pork*
- *155g (5oz) fresh water chestnuts*
- *2.5cm (1in) knob fresh ginger*
- *3 green (spring) onions, chopped*
- *12 baby eggplant (aubergine)*
- *1 cup (150g/5oz) potato flour*
- *3 cups (750ml/24fl oz) peanut oil, for deep-frying*
- SAUCE: *1 cup (250ml/8fl oz) light soy sauce*
- *1/2 cup (125ml/4fl oz) ponzu sauce, or lime juice*
- *1/4 cup (60ml/2fl oz) sake, for cooking*

Combine meats in a bowl. Peel chestnuts and ginger and chop finely; add green onion. (Alternatively, mince these 3 ingredients in a blender or food processor.) Stir into meat mixture. (Stuffing can be prepared ahead to this point and refrigerated until required.) Wash eggplant and cut each in quarters lengthways, keeping stem end intact. Place potato flour in a shallow dish. Dust inside of each eggplant with flour, tapping off excess. Take some of the meat and shape into a sausage.

WATER CHESTNUTS
Substitute canned water chestnuts if fresh are unavailable. Fresh water chestnuts take a little time to peel, but have a superior crunch.
POTATO FLOUR
Potato flour is available from health food shops and good delis. Pure cornflour can be substituted.
PONZU SAUCE
This citrus-flavoured sauce is available from Asian supermarkets, but lime juice is a good substitute.

Fill an eggplant with this and reshape it, with a little meat showing between each cut. Roll in potato flour, tap off excess. Stuff remaining eggplant in the same way. (Eggplant can be covered and refrigerated at this stage, for cooking later.)

Heat oil in a deep-frying pan. Heat oven to lowest temperature. Place a tray lined with absorbent paper in the oven. Fry eggplant, in batches, turning frequently, for about 8 minutes, or until meat is golden. Keep warm in oven. Serve with combined sauce ingredients, passed separately.

SEARED SCALLOPS ON RICE NOODLES WITH ASPARAGUS AND CHILLI SAUCE

- *3 bunches asparagus, spears trimmed and halved*
- *375g (12oz) rice noodles*
- *1 daikon, peeled and finely julienned*
- *4 green (spring) onions, cut thinly on the diagonal*
- *1 tablespoon sesame oil*
- *30 large scallops (some with roe attached)*

SAUCE: *1/2 cup (135g/4 1/2 oz) palm sugar, shaved or grated*
- *2 tablespoons sesame oil*
- *1 1/2 cups (375ml/12fl oz) fish stock*
- *3 tablespoons sweet chilli sauce*

Heat a large pot of water to boiling. Drop in asparagus, return to the boil and then remove asparagus immediately. Put noodles into boiling water, simmer for 3 minutes; drain through a colander. Immediately mix in daikon and green onion (reserve some green onion for garnish).

Simmer sauce ingredients in a small saucepan. Heat sesame oil in a frying pan over high heat. Sear scallops, in batches, for 1 minute each side. Arrange noodle mixture on serving plates, top with asparagus and scallops. Spoon hot sauce over, garnish with reserved green onion and serve immediately.

BLOOD ORANGE JELLY WITH TAMARILLO, STAR FRUIT AND VANILLA SYRUP

- *6 sheets gelatine*
- *2 cups (500ml/16fl oz) strained blood orange juice (or the juice from navel or valencia oranges)*
- *1 cup (220g/7oz) caster sugar*
- *1 vanilla pod*
- *1 thin-skinned lemon, sliced thinly*
- *6 tamarillos*
- *2 star fruit, thinly sliced*
- *Thick cream, to serve*

Soak gelatine in cold water for 5 minutes. Heat juice and half the sugar in a saucepan until simmering. Squeeze gelatine and stir into hot juice until dissolved. Pour into 6 timbale moulds or small glasses, each about 1/3 cup (80ml/2 1/2 fl oz). Cool, then refrigerate until set.
Halve vanilla pod lengthways, scrape out seeds into a saucepan. Add pod, 4 cups (1L/32fl oz) water, lemon and the remaining sugar and simmer, stirring until sugar dissolves. With a small sharp knife, cut a shallow X in the tip of each tamarillo. Place fruit in syrup. Cover and poach over low heat, turning fruit frequently for 15 minutes. Cool fruit in syrup, then peel. Boil poaching liquid until reduced by half. Cool.
To serve, dip each jelly mould into hot water for 10 seconds. Turn out onto serving plates. Arrange tamarillos and star fruit with jelly, then spoon sauce around. Pass cream separately.

Opposite: Seared Scallops on Rice Noodles with Asparagus and Chilli Sauce.

SUMMER

BREAKFAST
TO TAKE FISHING

SERVES SIX

ICY PINEAPPLE JUICE

Buy unsweetened pineapple juice, decant into plastic bottles and freeze. Take a chilled bottle of soda water if you prefer diluted juice.

...

LITTLE BACON-AND-EGG PIES

- 6 sheets ready-rolled puff pastry
- 6 tablespoons either Dijon or mild American mustard, tomato sauce or chutney
- 6 small eggs
- 6 thick rashers bacon, chopped
- 1/4 cup chopped chives
- 1/2 cup grated cheddar (optional)
- 1 egg yolk, extra, for glaze

Preheat oven to 190°C/375°F/Gas Mark 4. Lightly grease a baking tray. Using a saucer or pot lid as a guide, cut out 6 pastry rounds, each 20cm (8in) in diameter. Spread with mustard, sauce or chutney. Lay a pastry round in a shallow bowl. Break an egg into this 'nest' and sprinkle with bacon and chives (and cheese, if using). Season to taste with salt and black pepper. Bring edges together in centre, roll over a little and pinch to seal. Carefully lift pie onto baking tray. Repeat with remaining ingredients, spacing pies at least 2.5cm (1in) apart on tray. Bake for 25–30 minutes, or until golden and firm (check base of pastry). Cool, then store in an airtight container.

SANDWICHES OF POPPY SEED LOAF WITH CREAM CHEESE SPREAD

- 1/2 cup (125ml/4fl oz) milk
- 2 eggs
- Finely grated rind of 1 medium lemon
- 1/3 cup (80ml/2 1/2 fl oz) lemon juice
- 1/4 cup (30g/1oz) poppy seeds
- 185g (6oz) butter, at room temperature
- 3/4 cup (170g/5 1/2 oz) caster sugar
- 2 cups (300g/9 1/2oz) self-raising flour

Preheat oven to 180°C/350°F/Gas Mark 4. Grease a 25 x 11cm (10 x 4 1/2in) loaf tin and line base with baking paper. Whisk milk in a measuring jug with eggs, lemon rind, juice and poppy seeds (mixture will sour a little). Cream butter and sugar until pale and fluffy. Sift flour and 1/2 teaspoon of salt into another bowl.

Add flour and egg mixtures alternately to creamed butter and sugar, stirring after each addition until combined. Spoon batter into prepared tin and bake in centre of oven for 60 minutes, or until a skewer inserted in centre comes out clean.

Place loaf in tin on a wire rack and cool completely. Turn out and cut into slices 6mm (1/4in) thick, spread with cream cheese spread (recipe follows) and make sandwiches. Reshape loaf and wrap in a clean cloth. Place in an airtight container for transportation; refrigerate until required.

CREAM CHEESE SPREAD: Beat 100g (3 1/2oz) softened cream cheese with 45g (1 1/2oz) softened butter until smooth. Beat in finely grated rind and juice of 1 lemon and 1 cup (160g/5oz) sifted pure icing sugar until smooth.

Opposite: Little Bacon-and-Egg Pies.

BREAKFAST FOR A CELEBRATION

SERVES EIGHT

STRAWBERRIES WITH BROWN SUGAR AND CRÈME FRAÎCHE

- *4 punnets (1kg/2lb) strawberries*
- *200ml (6¹/₂ fl oz) crème fraîche or sour cream*
- *Finely grated rind of 1 lemon*
- *1 cup (200g/6¹/₂oz) dark brown sugar*
- *1 teaspoon ground cinnamon*

Rinse strawberries, if necessary, and drain. Leave hulls attached. Combine crème fraîche and lemon rind in a small serving bowl. Combine brown sugar and cinnamon in a similar bowl. Pile berries on a serving tray and pass with crème fraîche and sugar. Dip strawberries first in crème and then in sugar.

FIGS, RICOTTA, WALNUTS AND PROSCIUTTO ON TURKISH BREAD

- *1 long loaf Turkish bread, or 2 small round loaves*
- *16 thin slices prosciutto*
- *1¹/₄ cups (250g/8oz) fresh ricotta*
- *¹/₂ cup (60g/2oz) walnut pieces, roasted and chopped*
- *4 large figs (or 8 smaller), sliced*
- *Walnut oil (optional)*

Cut bread in half to give 2 long pieces or slice into 4 rounds. Cut each long piece into 8 or each round piece into 4 (16 pieces). Place under grill, crust-side-up, and toast lightly. Turn bread and top each piece with a slice of prosciutto, some ricotta, walnuts and a slice of fig. Drizzle with a little walnut oil, if using, and sprinkle with freshly ground black pepper, to taste. Grill until edges of bread are lightly coloured and ricotta is warm. Serve immediately.

. . .

ROCKMELON JUICE WITH MINT AND HONEY

Peel 3 rockmelons, discard seeds and process flesh in a blender or juice extractor. Stir in honey to taste. Stuff sprigs of fresh mint into a serving jug, add ice cubes and pour juice over. Refrigerate remaining juice until required to top up jug.

CRÈME FRAÎCHE
To make your own crème fraîche, combine equal quantities of sour cream and heavy cream. Stand at room temperature for 24 hours, or until thick. Transfer to a sterile container, cover and refrigerate.

Opposite: Figs, Ricotta, Walnuts and Prosciutto on Turkish Bread.

LAZY BRUNCH
ON THE VERANDAH

SERVES FOUR

CAFÉ AU LAIT

Serve either strong black coffee with a jug of steaming-hot milk in large cups, or black coffee in small cups and pass a bowl of pure cream. Float a spoonful of cream on top and sip the coffee through it.

. . .

RICOTTA GRIDDLE CAKES

- *2²/₃ cups (400g/13oz) self-raising flour*
- *6 eggs, whisked lightly*
- *1 ¹/₂ cups (375ml/12fl oz) milk*
- *1 ¹/₂ cups (300g/9¹/₂oz) fresh ricotta*
- *Butter, for cooking*

Sift flour and a pinch of salt into a mixing jug or bowl. Make a well in centre, add combined eggs and milk, stirring to mix. Stir in fresh ricotta. Cover mixing jug, or transfer mixture into a jug, cover and stand in cool place until required. To cook, heat a griddle or heavy-based, preferably non-stick, frying pan, until a drop of water sizzles when flicked onto the surface. (You will need to keep regulating the heat during cooking.) Crumple a piece of baking paper and lightly spread a small amount of butter over the hot griddle with it (take care not to push down too hard). Re-butter the griddle before cooking each batch. Pour mixture onto griddle to form 10–12cm (4–5in) diameter rounds. Fit as many rounds as you can in each batch. Cook until edges are crisp and bubbles appear on surface. Turn and cook undersides. Place in a single layer on a clean teatowel and cover with another teatowel. Repeat until you have the required amount.

CRISP PROSCIUTTO
AND BUTTERED SWEET CORN

To crisp prosciutto, place very thin slices (2–3 per person) in a single layer on baking paper in a grill tray. Cook under a hot grill until crisp, then transfer to a serving plate. Sweet corn is one of those precious ingredients best served with minimal fuss. Simply cut kernels from cob with a sharp knife. Place in a heavy-based frying pan with butter, salt and freshly ground black pepper to taste. Cook over low heat, stirring occasionally, for about 20 minutes. The rule of thumb is 1 cob of corn per person and as much butter as your conscience allows.

. . .

BLUEBERRIES AND NECTARINES
WITH HONEYCOMB AND
CINNAMON YOGHURT

Cut 4 nectarines from their stones and slice thinly. Place in a bowl with the juice of 1 lemon and 1 punnet (150g/5oz) of blueberries, rinsed and dried. Add 60g (2oz) honeycomb, cut into small cubes. Refrigerate until required. Combine 1 cup (250g/8oz) natural yoghurt with 1 teaspoon ground cinnamon. Pass with nectarines and serve as an alternative accompaniment to the warm Ricotta Griddle Cakes (recipe this page).

STONE FRUIT

As an alternative to nectarines, halve red plums, drizzle with honey, sprinkle with cinnamon and a few dots of butter, and bake in a medium oven until soft and sticky.

Opposite: Ricotta Griddle Cakes with
Crisp Prosciutto and Buttered Sweet Corn.

SLOW BRUNCH
WHILE SAILING

CHICKEN, MUSHROOM AND SEMI-DRIED TOMATO LOAF

- *250g (8oz) semi-dried tomato halves, drained of oil*
- *1kg (2lb) chicken tenderloin fillets*
- *200g (6¹/₂oz) small button mushrooms, thinly sliced*
- *¹/₄ cup chopped chervil or parsley*
- *¹/₄ cup chopped chives*
- *2 cups (140g/4¹/₂oz) fresh breadcrumbs (process any bread you like in a blender or food processor)*
- *¹/₂ cup (125ml/4fl oz) pouring cream*
- *1 tablespoon Dijon mustard*

Preheat oven to 170°C/340°F/Gas Mark 3. Lightly brush a 25 x 11cm (10 x 4¹/₂in) loaf tin with oil (from tomatoes). Place tomatoes, skin-side-down, in a single layer to cover base of tin. In a large bowl, combine remaining ingredients, except cream and mustard. Combine cream and mustard, season to taste with about 1 teaspoon of sea salt and black pepper. Stir through chicken mixture. Spoon into loaf tin, pressing down to pack firmly. Cover loosely with foil and bake in centre of oven for 1¹/₄ hours. Cool in tin, then refrigerate overnight. Turn out on a serving platter to slice (use a sharp serrated knife).

Opposite: Chicken, Mushroom and Semi-Dried Tomato Loaf.

SEMI-DRIED TOMATOES

Semi-dried tomatoes can be expensive to buy. To make your own, cut Roma (egg) tomatoes in half lengthways, place cut-side-up in a single layer on a non-reactive tray and bake at 160°C/325°F/Gas Mark 3 for 3–4 hours. Store covered in olive oil. The oil takes up the flavour and can be re-used for dressings, grills, frittata...whatever.

WHITE BEAN AND PARSLEY MASH

- *Extra virgin olive oil*
- *8 cloves garlic, peeled and slightly crushed*
- *2 or 3 cans, each 300g (9½oz),*
butter or small lima beans, drained and rinsed
(quantity depends on appetites of brunchers)
- *1 cup chopped parsley*
- *1 teaspoon sea salt*
- *Squeeze of lemon juice*

Warm ¼ cup (60ml/2fl oz) oil in a frying pan over the lowest possible heat. Add garlic and cook gently until cloves are just beginning to colour. Stir in beans and heat through gently. Stir in parsley and sea salt. Remove from heat and press mixture with a potato masher or the back of a spoon to give a coarse mash. Spoon into serving bowl and sprinkle with lemon juice, a little more olive oil and freshly ground black pepper to taste. Serve at room temperature with fresh or toasted Turkish bread.

LYCHEES AND CHERRIES ON ICE

Half-fill a deep container with ice. Top with stalks of mint, if you wish, and place combined cherries and lychees on top. Have another bowl available for seeds and skins.

...

MINTED HONEYDEW MELON

Cut a well-chilled honeydew melon into chunks and combine with a handful of torn mint leaves. Serve with Greek Yoghurt with Honeycomb and Nuts (recipe follows).

...

GREEK YOGHURT WITH HONEYCOMB AND NUTS

- *1 cup (125g/4oz) walnuts, lightly toasted and chopped*
- *2 tablespoons brown sugar*
- *1 teaspoon ground cinnamon*
- *500g (1lb) Greek-style natural yoghurt*
- *100g (3½oz) honeycomb,*
cut into about 6mm (½in) dice

Combine walnuts, sugar and cinnamon. Spoon yoghurt into a serving bowl. Sprinkle with nut mixture and pass honeycomb separately, or if space is limited, spoon yoghurt into a shallow dish and sprinkle with nut and honeycomb mixture.

...

GRAPE JUICE SPRITZER

- *2 x 750ml (24fl oz) bottles white muscatel pure grape juice*
- *1 x 750ml (24fl oz) bottle soda water*
- *Juice of 3 lemons, plus lemon slices, for garnish*

Have all ingredients chilled. Combine ingredients and serve over ice or frozen green grapes.

...

COFFEE OR TEA IN A FLASK

Make hot brewed tea or coffee and pour into a vacuum flask. Pack mugs, spoons, milk and sugar.

Morning Tea
AT THE CRICKET

| Serves six

RASPBERRIES
You'll find the best raspberry jam in country towns and at fêtes. Stock up when you come across it. Alternatively, try making your own, using frozen raspberries. Late-season raspberries drop dramatically in price, so be generous with them.

TINY SCONES WITH PURE RASPBERRY JAM AND MASCARPONE

- *2 cups (300g/9¹/₂oz) self-raising flour*
- *1 teaspoon caster sugar*
- *1 tablespoon butter*
- *Finely grated rind of 1 small lemon*
- *¹/₃ cup (80ml/2¹/₂fl oz) milk*
- *Milk and caster sugar, extra*
- *Good-quality raspberry jam and mascarpone, to serve*

Preheat oven to 220°C/450°F/Gas Mark 6. Lightly grease a baking tray. Sift flour and ¹/₄ teaspoon salt into a mixing bowl. Stir in sugar. Rub in butter until mixture resembles breadcrumbs. Stir in rind and add milk combined with ¹/₃ cup (80ml/2¹/₂fl oz) cold water, to give a soft dough. (Add a little more water if mixture is too dry.) Turn out on a lightly floured work surface and gently knead into a ball. Press out into a disc 2.5cm (1in) thick. Using a 2.5cm (1in) cutter or small glass, cut into rounds. Place scones on prepared baking tray. Brush with milk and sprinkle with caster sugar. Bake in centre of oven for 10 minutes. Wrap in a cloth or napkin while slightly warm. Pack with the very best raspberry jam you can find, a jar of mascarpone and a small spreading knife.

Lemon Shortbread

- 250g (8oz) unsalted butter, at room temperature
- 1/2 cup (110g/3 1/2oz) caster sugar
- Finely grated rind and juice of 1 medium lemon
- 2 1/2 cups (375g/12oz) wholemeal plain flour
- 1 cup (160g/5 1/2oz) rice flour

LEMON ICING (OPTIONAL):
- 1/2 cup (80g/2 1/2oz) pure icing sugar, sifted
- 2 tablespoons lemon juice

Heat oven to 170°C/340°F/Gas Mark 3. Lightly grease an oven tray. Cream butter and sugar until pale and fluffy. Stir in lemon rind and juice, then flours. Knead until mixture clings together. Turn onto a work surface, roll out to 1cm (1/2in) thickness and, using a 5cm (2in) cutter or a glass, cut into rounds. Place on prepared oven tray. Press the blunt edge of a knife across the centre of each shortbread to score it lightly. Bake in centre of oven for 20–25 minutes, or until just beginning to colour. Cool on tray. For the icing, mix icing sugar with lemon juice until smooth then place in a small plastic bag. Squeeze icing into one corner of bag, twist bag to keep it there, and make a tiny snip with scissors across the pointed corner. Use this as a piping bag to drizzle icing on shortbreads. When icing is completely set, pack as many shortbreads as you need into an airtight carrying container. Any extra will keep well in an airtight container and can also be frozen.

Makes about 30.

Finger Sandwiches with Black Olive Tapenade and Egg

- 3 eggs, hard-boiled
- 1 tablespoon soft butter
- 60g (2oz) black olive tapenade, purchased either from bulk supply at a delicatessen, or in small jars of about 100g (3 1/2oz)
- 4 flat anchovy fillets (optional)
- 12 slices Cape-seed or Five-seed bread (or multi-grain bread)

Shell eggs, mash with butter and season to taste with salt and freshly ground black pepper. Combine tapenade with mashed anchovy fillets, if using. Spread 4 slices of bread with egg mixture. Place another slice of bread on top and spread this with tapenade. Top with remaining bread. Cut each sandwich into 3 fingers. Wrap in a slightly damp cloth napkin and pack into an airtight carrying container.

. . .

Minty Iced Tea in a Flask

Start preparation the day before. Cool 6 cups (1.5L/48fl oz) black tea to room temperature; pour some into an ice-cube tray and freeze. Refrigerate remainder. Place mint sprigs into a chilled flask, then tea ice-blocks. Pour in remaining chilled tea. Take lemon slices in a separate container and add to tea as a garnish. Serve in small glasses with sugar cubes offered separately.

Opposite: Lemon Shortbread and Finger Sandwiches with Black Olive Tapenade and Egg.

A SELECTION OF SAUSAGES

Choose a selection from a well-stocked deli: Italian pork, kransky, clobassy, Spanish chorizo, debriciner, saucisson, weisswurst. Be guided by the deli staff. Some of the firmer salami-style sausages require only heating, rather than cooking. The Italian pork must be well-cooked, so place this on barbecue toward the end of lamb cooking time. Place others on barbecue when lamb is resting. Cook sausages whole, then cut into large pieces and serve on a platter with cutlets.

...

ROASTED TOMATOES, RED ONION AND GARLIC

- *10–12 firm, ripe Roma (egg) tomatoes, quartered*
- *4 large red onions, peeled and cut into wedges*
- *1 head garlic, separated into cloves and peeled*
- *¼ cup (60ml/2fl oz) black pepper oil (or use olive oil and 1 tablespoon coarsely ground black pepper)*

Preheat oven to 180°C/350°F/Gas Mark 4. Place tomatoes, onion and garlic in a shallow non-reactive baking dish. Drizzle with oil. Sprinkle with pepper, if using. Bake for at least 1 hour. If more convenient, bake at 150°C/300°F/Gas Mark 2 for 2–3 hours. The tomatoes remain intact and look semi-dried; the onion will be soft and slightly charred. Serve warm with the sausages and lamb.

SORREL AND HALOUMI WEDGES

- *2 tablespoons butter*
- *¾ cup finely chopped eschallots, young white onions or green (spring) onions (in that order of preference)*
- *250g (8oz) sorrel leaves*
- *250g (8oz) haloumi cheese, cut into 6mm (¼in) cubes*
- *8 eggs*
- *1¼ cups (300ml/10fl oz) sour cream*
- *½ cup chopped Italian (flat-leaf) parsley*
- *¼ teaspoon freshly grated nutmeg*

Melt butter in a deep frying pan. Add eschallots, cover and cook, stirring occasionally, over medium heat. Wash sorrel; discard any tough stalks from larger leaves. Add to eschallots and stir for 1 minute.

Turn into a 20 x 30 x 2.5cm (8 x 12 x 1in) non-reactive ovenproof dish. Sprinkle cheese over sorrel mixture. (Refrigerate at this stage if preparing in advance.)

Preheat oven to 180°C/350°F/Gas Mark 4. Whisk eggs with sour cream, parsley and nutmeg and season to taste with salt and freshly ground black pepper. Pour over sorrel and bake for 1 hour, or until puffed and golden and set in the centre. Cut into slices and serve hot or at room temperature.

Raspberry Tart with Yoghurt Cream

PASTRY: *1 ⅓ cups (200g/6 ½oz) plain flour • ¾ cup (100g/3 ½oz) ground almonds (coarsely grind blanched almonds, if you can, for best texture and flavour; otherwise use packaged almond meal) • 30g (1oz) vanilla sugar • 150g (5oz) unsalted butter • 1 large egg, beaten lightly • 3 punnets (450g/14oz) raspberries • 1 punnet (150g/5oz) loganberries or blackberries • Icing sugar, to serve*

To make pastry, combine flour, almonds and vanilla sugar in a bowl. Rub in butter until mixture resembles coarse breadcrumbs. Stir in egg, then gather dough into a ball. Flatten into a disc, wrap in a piece of baking paper at least 40cm (16in) long and the full width of the roll. Refrigerate for at least 30 minutes. (If refrigerated overnight, the pastry will need to sit at room temperature for at least 30 minutes to soften.) Place parcel on work surface, open out paper and roll out pastry on this, to fit a 20 x 30cm (8 x 12in) rectangular flan tin or a 23cm (9in) round flan tin (tins should have a removable base). Lift pastry into tin, using paper to assist. Peel off paper and press pastry into base and along edges. It is soft and breaks easily. Piece it together and smooth with your fingers.

Trim edges and freeze shell for 5 minutes.

Preheat oven to 190°C/375°F/Gas Mark 4.

Prick base of crust with a fork and line with baking paper. Fill with baking weights, rice or dried beans and bake for 20 minutes. Remove from oven, carefully lift out paper and weights and return crust to oven for 5 minutes, or until base is dry and crisp.

Cool in tin on a wire rack.

Spread 1 cup (250ml/8fl oz) yoghurt cream (recipe follows) over base of crust. Scatter raspberries and other berries over. Refrigerate until required. Remove base of flan tin and slide tart onto serving plate (serve from the base if you feel safer). Dust with icing sugar. Pass remaining yoghurt cream separately.

YOGHURT CREAM: Lightly whip 1 ¼ cups (300ml/10fl oz) pouring cream. Stir in about 1 cup (250ml/8fl oz) good quality full-cream natural yoghurt. Sprinkle with 1 tablespoon brown sugar. Cover and refrigerate for several hours or overnight. Stir before serving.

· · ·

Didi's Lemon Tennis Drink

• *2 cups (500ml/16fl oz) water • 2 cups (440g/14oz) sugar • 1 tablespoon citric acid • 2 tablespoons lemon essence*

Bring water to the boil and dissolve sugar in the water. Stir in citric acid. Cool. Stir in lemon essence. Store in a sealed bottle. When required, combine base to taste with equal quantities of chilled lemonade and water.

LUNCH AT HOME WITH FRIENDS

SERVES SIX

ROASTED STICKY RED ONION TARTS WITH CHERVIL

- *4 medium red onions, unpeeled*
- *6 cloves garlic, peeled*
- *30g (1oz butter)*
- *½ cup (125ml/4fl oz) balsamic vinegar*
- *1 cup (250ml/8fl oz) full-cream natural yoghurt*
- *½ cup chervil, chopped (reserve 6 sprigs for garnish)*
- *Shaved parmesan, to serve*

PASTRY: *2 cups (300g/9½oz) plain flour*
- *1 teaspoon chilli powder*
- *1 cup (80g/3oz) grated parmesan (optional)*
- *60g (2oz) butter*
- *Juice of 1 medium lemon*

Preheat oven to 180°C/350°F/Gas Mark 4. Place whole onions and garlic cloves in a shallow oven dish and roast for 1 hour. Stand at room temperature. To make pastry, combine flour, chilli powder, parmesan and a pinch of salt in a bowl. Rub in butter until mixture resembles fine breadcrumbs. Stir in lemon juice and knead in enough chilled water to make a firm dough. Form into a flat disc, wrap in plastic wrap (film) or baking paper and refrigerate for at least 30 minutes, or until required.

CHERVIL

Chervil is a member of the parsley family and has a delicate aniseed flavour. It is not always easy to buy, but it will grow well from seed in the garden or in a pot. A small amount of finely chopped fennel leaves or crushed fennel seed can be substituted for chervil.

To make balsamic mixture, stir butter and vinegar in a small saucepan over low heat until butter has melted. Simmer for 5 minutes. Cut each onion into 8 wedges and peel carefully, keeping each wedge intact. Preheat oven to 220°C/450°F/Gas Mark 6. Lightly grease an oven tray. Divide pastry into 6 equal pieces, knead into balls and roll into 13cm (5in) circles. Place on oven tray. Arrange onion and garlic on each pastry circle and pinch up edges of pastry to form a rim. Spoon a little balsamic mixture over each tart and bake for 15–20 minutes, or until pastry is golden and crisp. Remove from oven and place tarts on serving plates. Brush with remaining balsamic mixture. Combine yoghurt and chervil and spoon a dollop onto each tart. Garnish with shaved parmesan and chervil sprigs.

Opposite: Roasted Sticky Red Onion Tarts with Chervil.

BAKED HAM

- *1 leg ham, about 5–6 kg (10–12lb)*
- *About 50 whole cloves, for garnish*
- *About 24 slices purchased glacé orange, for garnish*
- GLAZE: *Juice of 2 oranges*
- *²/₃ cup (140g/4¹/₂oz) brown sugar*
- *2 tablespoons Dijon mustard*

To remove skin from ham, cut a zig-zag line around shank, right through the skin. Slip a sharp knife between skin and fat at the thick end of the ham. Loosen skin enough for you to push your fingers under it. Taking care not to break the fat layer, work the skin loose with your fingers. Remove it in one piece and discard.

Combine glaze ingredients in a small saucepan and stir over medium heat until sugar dissolves. Simmer for 5 minutes. Meanwhile, using a very sharp knife, cut a 2.5cm (1in) diamond pattern into the fat. Take care to cut through only the very top layer of fat. You should not cut through to the meat or fat will spread during cooking. Arrange cloves and glacé orange on ham in a decorative pattern (secure each orange slice with a clove).

Adjust shelves in oven to accommodate ham. Preheat oven to 180°C/350°F/Gas Mark 4.

Place ham on a rack positioned over a baking tray. Brush liberally with some of the warm glaze. Pour hot water into baking tray to cover base by about 1cm (¹/₂in). Bake, brushing frequently with glaze, for 30–40 minutes. The ham is already cooked, so this is merely a warming and glazing process. Do not be tempted to heat the ham any longer as it will dry out. Remove from oven and stand at room temperature until required. The ham is best carved just before serving.

Any remaining ham on the bone should be wrapped in a clean cloth and refrigerated or kept in a cool place.

ROASTED TOMATO RELISH

- *2kg (4lb) Roma (egg) tomatoes*
- *2 bulbs garlic, unpeeled*
- *1 medium red onion, finely diced*
- *¹/₄ cup (60ml/2fl oz) balsamic vinegar*
- *¹/₂ (125ml/4fl oz) cup olive oil*
- *1 teaspoon coarsely ground black pepper*
- *¹/₂ cup chopped Italian (flat-leaf) parsley*

Preheat oven to 180°C/350°F/Gas Mark 4.

Cut tomatoes in half lengthways. Place, cut-side-up, on a baking tray. Bake for 1 hour. Add unpeeled bulbs of garlic and bake for a further 20 minutes, or until garlic is soft. Remove from oven, chop tomatoes and place in a serving bowl with juices and remaining ingredients. Squeeze garlic from skins and stir through tomato mixture. Refrigerate until required.

PASHKA WITH ALMOND BREAD AND MIXED BERRIES

- *500g (1lb) cream cheese, at room temperature*
- *125g (4oz) unsalted butter, at room temperature*
- *2 egg yolks*
- *1 cup (160g/5oz) pure icing sugar, sifted*
- *1 teaspoon vanilla essence*
- *²/₃ cup (100g/3¹/₂oz) slivered almonds, roasted until golden*
- *²/₃ cup (150g/5oz) mixed glacé fruit (peaches, apricots, citron, quince), diced*
- *Almond bread, to serve (recipe follows)*
- *Fresh berries, to serve*

Using an electric mixer, beat cream cheese with butter
and egg yolks until fluffy. Beat in sugar and fold
in remaining ingredients.

Line a 4-cup (1L/32fl oz) charlotte tin or similar
shape, or 8 timbale moulds or small glasses, each
about ¹/₂ cup (125ml/4fl oz), with a double thickness
of damp muslin, leaving a generous overhang. Spoon
cheese mixture into mould(s), cover with plastic and
refrigerate for several hours, or until set firm.

To serve, turn pashka out of mould(s) using the
muslin overhang to pull. Remove muslin. Place large
pashka on a serving plate, sliced, with almond bread
and berries; serve small pashka, unsliced, on
individual plates with almond bread and berries.

ALMOND BREAD

- *3 egg whites*
- *¹/₂ cup (110g/3¹/₂oz) caster sugar*
- *²/₃ cup (100g/3oz) plain flour*
- *1 cup (100g/3oz) blanched almonds*

Preheat oven to 180°C/350°F/Gas Mark 4.
Grease a 8cm x 25cm (3in x 10in) bar tin and line
base with baking paper. Using an electric mixer, beat
egg whites until firm peaks form, add sugar and beat
for 10 minutes until sugar dissolves. Fold in sifted
flour and walnuts, spoon into bar tin and smooth top.

Bake for 45–55 minutes until golden and firm
to touch. Stand in tin for 10 minutes, then turn out
onto a wire rack until completely cold. Using
a serrated knife, slice bread as thinly as possible.
Place slices in a single layer in an oven tray and bake
at 120°C/250°F/Gas Mark 1 for 15–20 minutes,
or until pale golden and crisp. Cool completely, then
store in an airtight container for up to two weeks.
Makes about 60 slices.

SUBTLY SPICED DINNER IN THE GARDEN

SERVES SIX

ROASTED CAPSICUM
WITH GARLIC ANCHOVY PASTE
ON TOASTED BRIOCHE

- *4 yellow, red or orange capsicums (bell peppers)*
- *8 cloves garlic, peeled*
- *1 cup (250ml/8fl oz) milk*
- *20 anchovy fillets, in oil (2 x 45g/1¹/₂oz tins)*
- *1 tablespoon butter*
- *6 slices sweet (yellow) brioche, 6mm (¹/₂in) thick, toasted and cut into fingers*
- *24 rocket leaves*

DRESSING:

- *¹/₂ cup (125ml/4fl oz) reserved capsicum juice*
- *¹/₄ cup (60ml/2fl oz) lemon juice*
- *2 tablespoons olive oil*

ROASTING CAPSICUM

There are many theories about roasting and peeling capsicum (bell peppers). The method used here results in softly cooked capsicum. Grilling under or over a direct flame works well, but is messier. Placing hot capsicums in a covered bowl finishes the process by steaming and loosening the skin. The precious juices are caught in the bowl and can be used to reinforce the roasted capsicum flavour in the recipe.

Preheat oven to 190°C/375°F/Gas Mark 4. Quarter capsicum, pull out seeds and membrane. Place quarters on an oven tray, skin-side-up, and roast for about 20 minutes, or until skin is blackened and blistered. Transfer to a deep bowl, cover with a plate and cool until easy to handle. Peel capsicum and cut into thin strips. Keep with capsicum juices in covered bowl at room temperature, until required.

To make paste, place garlic and milk in a saucepan. Cook, uncovered, over low heat for 35 minutes, or until garlic is soft and milk has been reduced to about a quarter of the original amount. Drain anchovies (reserve oil for some other use). Add anchovies and butter to garlic mixture and stir over low heat for 10 minutes, or until mixture forms a paste. Turn into a small bowl or small, clean saucepan. Whisk dressing ingredients together. To serve, heat paste gently in a saucepan or microwave oven. Spread thickly on brioche and arrange on individual plates with roasted capsicum and rocket leaves. Spoon dressing over.

Opposite: Roasted Capsicum with Garlic Anchovy Paste on Toasted Brioche.

Barbecued or Roasted Leg of Lamb, Stuffed with Mint and Date Paste

- *12 fresh dates, stoned and chopped*
- *1 small red onion, finely diced*
- *½ cup each chopped mint, Italian (flat-leaf) parsley and coriander (cilantro) leaves*
- *Grated rind and juice of 1 lemon*
- *2 boned legs of lamb, each about 1.4 kg (2¾ lb)*
- *Olive oil*

Combine dates, onion, herbs and lemon rind and juice in a blender or food processor and work to a coarse paste. Open out legs of lamb and spread paste over the inside surface. Sprinkle generously with coarsely ground black pepper. Re-form legs and tie securely with kitchen string. Refrigerate until required. Stand for 30 minutes at room temperature before cooking.

Preheat oven to 250°C/525°F/Gas Mark 7, or prepare a hot barbecue. Place lamb on a rack positioned over an ovenproof baking dish (or barbecue-proof dish). Brush lightly with olive oil. Roast for 20 minutes in oven or covered barbecue. Reduce oven temperature to 180°C/350°F/Gas Mark 4, or open barbecue, closing it again as coals burn down. Cook for 40 minutes more (rare), or 60 minutes more (medium). Stand, covered with foil, in a warm place for at least 10 minutes before carving.

Sugar Snap Peas and Pea Sprouts

- *500g (1 lb) sugar snap peas, trimmed and strings removed*
- *Small punnet, about 150g (5oz) snow pea sprouts (mangetout sprouts)*
- *2 tablespoons walnut or light sesame oil*
- *1 tablespoon lemon juice*

Wash peas, drop into boiling water and return to the boil. Immediately drain through a colander, put into a serving bowl and cool to room temperature. Trim tough stalks from sprouts and add to cooled peas. Combine walnut oil and lemon juice and sprinkle dressing over salad.

Couscous in Buttery Veal and Saffron Stock

- *2 cups (500ml/16fl oz) veal stock*
- *¼ teaspoon saffron threads*
- *60g (2oz) butter*
- *250g (8oz) instant couscous*

Place stock, saffron threads and butter in a deep saucepan. Heat until simmering. Stir in couscous. Cover pan and turn off heat. Stand for 5 minutes, or until liquid is absorbed. Fluff up with a fork before serving.

SAFFRON

Saffron threads are the stigmas from the purple crocus flower. Because they are hand-picked and then dried, and about 4500 are needed for each gram, saffron is the world's most expensive spice. Powdered saffron does not have the quality of threads and is more effective as a colouring agent than for flavouring.

SORBET

Peach sorbet can be made using the peach poaching liquid and extra peaches, puréed.

POACHED PEACHES SERVED WITH RASPBERRY SORBET

- *6–8 firm ripe yellow peaches*
(make sure they are free of bruises)
- *Fresh raspberries, to decorate*

SYRUP: *1 cup (220g/7oz) caster sugar*
- *1 vanilla pod, split lengthways*
- *1 lemon, thinly sliced and seeds discarded*
- *1 tablespoon orange flower water*

Heat 4 cups (1L/32fl oz) water in a deep frying pan. Add syrup ingredients and simmer. Add whole peaches and, using a rubber spatula, turn to coat with liquid. Cover pan and simmer for 20 minutes, turning peaches often, but cook mostly with stem ends down. Remove peaches from liquid with a slotted spoon. Cool on a plate, then slip off skins. Keep at room temperature until required.

Boil poaching liquid until reduced and thickened. Cool. Serve peaches with Raspberry Sorbet (recipe follows), poaching liquid spooned over, and decorated with fresh raspberries.

RASPBERRY SORBET

- *1 cup (220g/7oz) caster sugar*
- *1 cup (250ml/8fl oz) freshly puréed raspberries*
- *Finely grated rind of 1 lemon*
- *1 egg white*

Combine sugar and 1 cup (250ml/8fl oz) water in a saucepan. Heat, stirring, until sugar dissolves. Skim off any froth and boil for 1 minute. Cool; refrigerate until required.

Combine syrup, purée and rind. Whisk egg white until soft peaks form and stir into syrup mixture until thoroughly combined. Pour into ice-cream machine and churn for 25–35 minutes, or until firm. Spoon into a shallow container, cover and freeze. Alternatively, pour mixture into a shallow freezer container, freeze until sludgy, stir with a fork and re-freeze until sludgy. Stir again. Repeat this another 4 times. Cover and freeze. About 30 minutes before serving, transfer from freezer to fridge to soften.

ICE-CREAM AFTER DARK

CARAMEL SUNDAES WITH WALNUTS AND CINNAMON

- *Good-quality purchased vanilla ice-cream*
- *Whipped cream or yoghurt cream (see raspberry tart recipe p61)*

CARAMEL: *60g (2oz) butter*
- *³/4 cup (150g/5oz) brown sugar*
- *½ cup (125ml/4fl oz) pouring cream*

TOPPING: *1 tablespoon ground cinnamon*
- *1 tablespoon caster sugar*
- *½ cup (60g/2 oz) chopped walnuts or pecans*

To make caramel, combine butter and brown sugar in a saucepan and stir over medium heat until sugar dissolves. Slowly add cream, stirring until mixture is smooth. Pour into a jug to cool. The caramel thickens as it cools. Combine topping ingredients. To serve, scoop ice-cream into a glass or dish, top with whipped cream and caramel. Sprinkle topping mixture over and serve immediately.

Opposite: Caramel Sundaes with Walnuts and Cinnamon.

LEMON STAR ANISE SORBET

- *1 cup (220g/7oz) caster sugar*
- *3 whole star anise*
- *1 cup (250ml/8fl oz) fresh lemon juice*
- *Finely grated rind of 2 small lemons*
- *1 egg white*

Combine sugar, star anise and 1 cup (250ml/8fl oz) water in a saucepan. Heat, stirring, until sugar dissolves. Skim off any froth and boil syrup for 1 minute. Cool; refrigerate until required. Combine strained syrup, juice and rind. Whisk egg white until soft peaks form and stir into syrup until thoroughly combined. Pour into ice-cream machine and churn for 25–35 minutes, or until firm. Spoon into a shallow container, cover and freeze. Alternatively, pour mixture into shallow freezer container, freeze until sludgy, stir with a fork and re-freeze until sludgy. Stir again. Repeat this another 4 times. Cover and freeze. About 30 minutes before serving, transfer from freezer to fridge to soften.

STAR ANISE

Whole star anise are the aromatic aniseed-flavoured seed pods of a small evergreen tree of the Magnolia family, native to China. It can be bought whole or as a ground ingredient in Five-Spice powder. Both are available from Asian supermarkets.

BROWNIES

- *125g (4oz) dark cooking chocolate*
- *125g (4oz) unsalted butter*
- *1 cup (200g/6¹/₂oz) brown sugar*
- *1 cup (125g/4oz) walnut pieces*
- *¹/₂ cup (75g/2¹/₂oz) self-raising flour*
- *1 teaspoon vanilla essence*
- *2 eggs*
- *Icing sugar, to serve*

Preheat oven to 180°C/350°F/Gas Mark 4. Lightly
grease a 20cm (8in) square cake tin and line base with
baking paper. Melt combined chocolate and butter in
a bowl over simmering water or in a microwave oven.
Combine sugar, walnuts and flour in a mixing bowl.
Add vanilla to chocolate and stir into mixed dry
ingredients. Lightly whisk eggs and stir into mixture.
Pour into cake tin and bake for 35–40 minutes,
or until brownie is firm to touch. The centre will still
be a little moist, but will solidify as brownie cools.
Cool in tin. Cut into 5cm (2in) squares
and serve dusted with icing sugar.
Makes 16 squares.

STRAWBERRY SORBET

- *1 cup (220g/7oz) caster sugar*
- *1 cup (250ml/8fl oz) freshly puréed strawberries*
- *Finely grated rind of 1 lemon*
- *1 egg white*

Combine sugar and 1 cup (250ml/8fl oz) water
in a saucepan. Heat, stirring, until sugar dissolves.
Skim off any froth and boil syrup for 1 minute.
Cool; refrigerate until required.
Combine syrup, purée and rind. Whisk egg white
until soft peaks form and stir into syrup until
thoroughly combined. Pour into ice-cream machine
and churn for 25–35 minutes, or until firm.
Spoon into a shallow container, cover and freeze.
Alternatively, pour mixture into shallow freezer
container, freeze until sludgy, stir with a fork and
re-freeze until sludgy. Stir again. Repeat this another
4 times. Cover and freeze. About 30 minutes before
serving, transfer from freezer to fridge to soften.

SUPPER PICNIC ON A PERSIAN RUG AT FULL MOON

SERVES SIX

TURKISH COFFEE

- *2 cups of water*
- *2 tablespoons sugar*
- *3 tablespoons of Turkish coffee*

Boil water in a small saucepan or Turkish coffee pot, with sugar (more or less to taste). Add Turkish coffee and return to heat. When coffee froths up to the rim, remove from heat and let the grounds settle. Repeat heating process twice more. Serve as soon as grounds have settled for the last time. For a spicier coffee, add a cardamon pod, a couple of cloves, a small cinnamon stick, or a pinch of freshly grated nutmeg to the water at the first boil.

FRESH DATES FILLED WITH PISTACHIO AND HONEY PASTE

- *³/₄ cup (100g/3¹/₂oz) pistachio kernels, coarsely ground*
- *1 tablespoon honey*
- *1 tablespoon lemon juice*
- *18 fresh dates, stones removed*

Combine pistachios with honey and juice to form a thick paste. Fill each date with the mixture and press cavity closed. Serve on a platter with Glazed Almonds and Walnuts (recipe next page) and purchased Turkish Delight. (Dates keep well, refrigerated, in a sealed container.)

PICNIC COFFEE

Take a gas ring, coffee pot and a bottle of water with you, to make the Turkish coffee or a strong black. Pack hot milk in a vacuum flask (thermos) if you wish. Serve the coffee in small cups or heat-proof glasses.

GLAZED ALMONDS AND WALNUTS

- *³/₄ cup (190ml/6fl oz) honey*
- *Finely grated rind of 1 lemon*
- *1 tablespoon lemon juice*
- *About 2 cups (250g/8oz) mixed walnut halves and raw almonds*
- *1 cup (220g/7oz) caster sugar*
- *Canola oil, for frying*
(about 1½ cups/375ml/12fl oz)

Combine honey, lemon rind and juice. Stir in nuts and stand, stirring occasionally, for about 2 hours. Spread sugar on a large plate. Drain nuts and toss in sugar to coat. Heat oil in a frying pan. Shallow-fry nuts, in batches, until just golden. Remove with a slotted metal spoon to a wire rack positioned over a tray to catch the drips. Cool; store in an airtight container.

TART OF ROAST PEACH WITH WALNUT CARDAMOM CRUST

- *4 firm ripe yellow peaches*
- *2 tablespoons brown sugar*
- *2 teaspoons orange flower water*
- *³/₄ cup (200ml/6fl oz) crème fraîche or sour cream*
- *2 tablespoons chopped roasted walnuts*

WALNUT CARDAMOM CRUST:
- *1 cup (150g/5oz) plain flour*
- *2 teaspoons ground cardamom*
- *½ cup (60g/2oz) ground walnuts*
- *2 tablespoons brown sugar*
- *125g (4oz) butter, diced*

Preheat oven to 170°C/340°F/Gas Mark 3. Line a shallow baking tray with baking paper. Halve and quarter peaches and remove stones. Place, skin-side-down, in a single layer on prepared tray. Sprinkle with brown sugar. Bake for 1–1½ hours. Stand at room temperature until required (can stand overnight, but transfer to a covered container). To make pastry, combine dry ingredients in a bowl and rub in butter until mixture clings together. Press into a flat disc, wrap in baking paper and refrigerate for 30 minutes.

Preheat oven to 190°C/375°F/Gas Mark 4. Roll out pastry on the paper to fit a 23cm (9in) flan tin with removable base. The pastry is soft, so lift it on the paper, press it into tin and peel off paper. Patch holes with your fingers. Trim edges, then freeze pastry for 5 minutes. Line with baking paper, fill with rice or dry beans and bake blind. Bake for 20 minutes, remove from oven, remove paper and weights and return pastry shell to centre of oven for 5 minutes, or until base is dry and crisp. Cool in tin.

When required, stir orange flower water into crème fraîche and spread over base of tart. Arrange baked peaches on top and sprinkle with chopped roasted walnuts. Transport tart in tin. Remove ring and serve from the metal base.

Opposite: Tart of Roast Peach with Walnut Cardamom Crust.

AUTUMN

SOUFFLÉS FOR BRUNCH

SERVES EIGHT

RICOTTA AND CHERVIL SOUFFLÉS WITH BACON AND MUSHROOMS

- *800g (26oz) Swiss brown or pine mushrooms*
- *16 thick slices bacon*

RICOTTA AND CHERVIL SOUFFLÉS:
- *60g (2oz) butter*
- *1 cup (150g/5oz) plain flour*
- *2 cups (500ml/16fl oz) milk*
- *6 eggs, separated (2 extra whites from custard recipe can be added, for larger volume)*
- *2 1/2 cups (500g/1lb) fresh ricotta, drained*
- *1 cup chervil, chopped roughly*

Preheat oven to 200°C/400°F/Gas Mark 5 with shelf positioned in lower third of oven. Lightly grease 6 x 1-cup (250ml/8fl oz) soufflé dishes. If you wish, tie a collar of baking paper around each dish. Position the paper about 5cm (2in) above rim of dish and tie securely with string. This allows the soufflé to rise high without spilling over edge of dish. (If you are incorporating extra egg whites, always use a collar.) For soufflés, melt butter in a deep saucepan over low heat. Stir in flour and cook for 2–3 minutes. Remove from heat and slowly whisk in milk; continue whisking until fairly smooth. Return to heat and cook, stirring, for about 3 minutes, or until mixture is thick. Remove from heat, cool. Stir in yolks, ricotta and chervil; season to taste with salt and freshly ground black pepper. (Mixture can be refrigerated at this stage for up to 2 days; bring to room temperature before continuing.)

Opposite: Ricotta and Chervil Soufflés with Bacon and Mushrooms.

Place prepared dishes on a shallow baking tray. Whisk egg whites to firm peaks, and fold them into base mixture until well incorporated, but still a little lumpy. Spoon carefully into prepared dishes, up to the top if using extra whites and a collar, slightly below rim if not. Cook for 25 minutes, or until soufflés have risen and are golden. Meanwhile, grill or fry bacon and mushrooms. Keep warm. Arrange bacon and mushrooms on serving plates. Remove soufflés from oven; cut string and carefully peel off paper. Place dishes on plates and serve immediately.

...

COMPOTE OF AUTUMN FRUITS WITH WARM HONEY CUSTARD

- *1/2 cup (100g/3 1/2oz) brown sugar*
- *1 vanilla pod, split lengthways*

FRUIT: *6 tamarillos, 3 pears (Beurre Bosc, Sensation, Corella), 2 guavas, 6 feijoas, 3 plums, 1 lemon*

Heat combined sugar, vanilla and 4 cups (1L/32fl oz) water in a deep frying pan until sugar dissolves. Cut an X on end of each tamarillo. Halve or quarter pears, depending on size. Slice guavas and feijoas thickly. Halve and stone plums and slice lemon thinly. Simmer fruit in syrup, covered, over low heat for 15 minutes. Turn off heat. To serve, carefully peel skin from tamarillos. Transfer fruit to a serving bowl. Reduce syrup in pan by half and pour over fruit. Serve with warm honey custard.

WARM HONEY CUSTARD: Whisk 1/2 cup (125ml/ 4fl oz) honey with 4 egg yolks in a bowl over simmering water, until thick. Stir in 2 cups (500ml/ 16fl oz) milk, stirring for 10 minutes, or until custard coats the back of a wooden spoon. Do not boil. Remove from heat and pour into a serving jug.

BRUNCH TO LINGER OVER

| SERVES EIGHT

SLOW-BAKED RUBY QUINCES

- 4–6 quinces, (about 1.5–2kg/3–4lb) peeled and cored
- 1 cup (220g/7oz) caster sugar
- 1 vanilla pod, split
- 1 lemon, sliced thinly
- 1 cinnamon stick

Preheat oven to 100°C/200°F/Gas Mark 1. Combine all ingredients in an ovenproof saucepan. Add water to cover and bring to the boil. Cover and bake overnight (8–10 hours). Can be left in turned-off oven until brunch time. Serve warm with Creamy Baked Lemon Rice (recipe below) and some syrup spooned over.

. . .

CREAMY BAKED LEMON RICE, STUDDED WITH CURRANTS

- ³/₄ cup (150g/5oz) short-grain rice
- ¹/₂ cup (75g/2¹/₂oz) currants
- Finely grated rind of 1 lemon
- ¹/₂ cup (100g/3¹/₂oz) brown sugar
- 1 teaspoon vanilla essence
- ¹/₂ cup (125ml/4fl oz) pouring cream
- 4 cups (1L/32fl oz) milk
- 30g (1oz) butter

Preheat oven to 100°C/200°F/Gas Mark 1. Wash rice under cold water, drain. Combine with currants, rind, sugar, vanilla, cream and milk in a 6-cup (1.5L/ 48fl oz) shallow ovenproof dish. Dot top with butter. Cover loosely with foil. Cook overnight (8–10 hours) in oven with quinces. After 8 hours, check pudding. Stir if still quite runny and cook, uncovered, until firm. Can be left in turned-off oven until brunch time.

Opposite: Toasted Brioche Fingers with Saffron Butter, Spinach Yoghurt and Grilled Prosciutto Ribbons.

SLOW-ROASTED ROMA TOMATOES

Halve 8 Roma (egg) tomatoes and place in a single layer in an ovenproof dish. Roast with ruby quinces.

TOASTED BRIOCHE FINGERS WITH SAFFRON BUTTER, SPINACH YOGHURT AND GRILLED PROSCIUTTO RIBBONS

- 125g (4oz) butter
- 2 teaspoons saffron threads
- 16 thin slices prosciutto
- 1 bunch English spinach, washed, dried and cut into thin ribbons
- 2 cups (500g/1lb) natural plain yoghurt
- 1 loaf sweet brioche, cut into thick slices and toasted

Melt butter in a small saucepan over low heat. Add saffron and stir for 1 minute; turn off heat. Cook prosciutto in a non-stick frying pan. Keep warm in oven. Add spinach to pan and stir over low heat for 5 minutes, or until wilted but still bright green. Season to taste with salt and freshly ground black pepper. Turn off heat and add yoghurt. To serve, cut toasted brioche into long fingers. Arrange on plates with spinach mixture and prosciutto. Drizzle warm saffron butter over toast. Serve immediately with Slow-Roasted Roma Tomatoes (recipe above).

. . .

SLICED FIGS, DIPPED IN QUINCE SYRUP

- 8–10 firm, ripe figs
- 2–3 cups quince cooking liquid (from Slow-Baked Ruby Quinces recipe)

Slice figs and arrange on a serving platter. Boil quince syrup in a saucepan until reduced to about one-third the volume and thickening. Pour into a small bowl and serve with figs.

MORNING TEA WHILE MUSHROOM PICKING

HOT MOCHA MILK

Combine drinking chocolate and good coffee to taste.
Mix with very hot milk and transport in a vacuum flask.

...

CHOC-CHOC BISCUITS

- *¼ cup (60ml/2fl oz) walnut or canola oil*
- *1 cup (200g/6½oz) brown sugar*
- *2 large eggs*
- *1½ cups (225g/7oz) plain flour*
- *⅓ cup (40g/1½oz) cocoa*
- *1 teaspoon baking soda*
- *250g (8oz) chocolate chips*
- *100g (3½oz) dark chocolate*

Preheat oven to 190°C/375°F/Gas Mark 4.
Lightly grease 2 baking trays. Using an electric mixer,
whisk oil, sugar and eggs until pale and smooth.
Add combined sifted flour, cocoa and baking soda.
Stir in chocolate chips. Take tablespoonfuls of
mixture, roll into balls and place on prepared baking
trays 2.5cm (1in) apart. Bake for 10–12 minutes,
or until firm. Cool on trays; transfer to a wire rack.
When cold, melt chocolate and place in a small plastic
bag. Squeeze chocolate into one corner of bag, twist
top to secure it and snip the corner of bag with scissors
to make a small hole. Drizzle chocolate
over biscuits. Leave until set.
Makes about 25.

*Opposite: Choc-Choc Biscuits and
Walnut Vanilla Icing Sugar Biscuits.*

BRIOCHE WITH FRUITED CREAM CHEESE

- *1 loaf sweet brioche*
- *1¼ cups (250g/8oz) cream cheese, at room temperature*
- *Strained juice of 1 orange*
- *1 cup (200g/6½oz) dried fruit medley*

Slice brioche and wrap or place in sealed container.
Beat cream cheese and orange juice in electric mixer
until smooth and light. Stir in fruit medley.
Spoon into a lidded container for transportation
to picnic site. Refrigerate until ready to pack.

...

WALNUT VANILLA ICING SUGAR BISCUITS

- *250g (8oz) butter, at room temperature*
- *½ cup (110g/3½oz) vanilla sugar*
- *1⅔ cups (200g/6½oz) walnuts*
- *2½ cups (375g/12oz) plain flour*
- *Pure icing sugar*

Preheat oven to 160°C/325°F/Gas Mark 3. Line
baking trays with baking paper. Cream butter and
sugar until pale and fluffy. Process walnuts to a fine
meal in a food processor or nut grinder. Stir into
butter with flour to make a stiff dough. Roll walnut-
size pieces of dough into crescent shapes and place on
baking trays. Bake for 20 minutes, or until firm
(biscuits should be barely golden). Leave on trays
until just warm, then dredge with icing sugar, coating
both sides. When cold, lift biscuits, still on paper,
into an airtight container.
Makes about 30.

FRESHLY BAKED FOR MORNING TEA

SPICED BUNS WITH CINNAMON MASCARPONE

- 2 cups (300g/9½oz) currants
- Finely grated rind and juice of 2 oranges
- 2 cups (500ml/16fl oz) milk
- 60g (2oz) unsalted butter, cut into small cubes
- 2 tablespoons nut oil (walnut, hazelnut), or canola oil
- ½ cup (110g/3½oz) raw sugar
- ½ teaspoon ground cinnamon
- ¼ teaspoon grated nutmeg
- ½ teaspoon salt
- 14g (½oz) dry yeast
- 2 eggs, beaten lightly
- 5½–6 cups (825–900g/27–30oz) plain flour, sifted

GLAZE: 1 tablespoon vanilla sugar
- 1 teaspoon gelatine

Heat currants with orange rind and juice in a small saucepan just to simmering point. Cool.
Heat milk almost to simmering point, add butter, oil, sugar, spices and salt, and stir until butter has melted.
Cool until barely warm. Stir yeast into ⅓ cup (80ml/2½fl oz) warm water in a small bowl.
Stand for about 5 minutes, or until foamy.
In a large bowl combine currant and milk mixtures, eggs and yeast mixture. Mix well, then gradually add flour, mixing with a dough hook of electric mixer or kneading by hand for about 10 minutes, or until the dough is smooth and elastic.

SPICED BUNS

You can make spiced buns ahead of time and freeze.
Reheat buns in a low oven for about 15 minutes.

CINNAMON MASCARPONE

Stir orange juice and finely grated rind into the cinnamon mascarpone to give it a change of personality.

You may need to add up to 1 cup flour extra, depending on the humidity of the day. Turn dough out on a floured board or tray, cover with a clean, damp tea towel and stand in a draft-free place for 1 hour, or until doubled in bulk.
Grease 2 baking trays (or dishes) lightly. Divide dough into 24 pieces of equal size. Knead each into a ball and position 12 on each tray, about 6mm (¼in) apart. Cover with a damp cloth and stand in a warm place for 30–40 minutes, or until doubled in bulk.
Preheat oven to 190°C/375°F/Gas Mark 4.
Bake buns in centre of oven for 20 minutes, or until golden. Dissolve glaze ingredients in 1 tablespoon hot water and brush on surface of hot buns.
Serve warm with cinnamon mascarpone.
CINNAMON MASCARPONE: Add 1 teaspoon ground cinnamon and ½ teaspoon grated nutmeg to 1¼ cups (250g/8oz) mascarpone and mix until smooth.
Makes 24.

Opposite: Spicy Buns with Cinnamon Mascarpone.

Warm Almond and Marzipan Tart

Pastry: *1/2 cup (60g/2oz) finely ground almonds*
- *1 1/2 cups (225g/7oz) plain flour*
- *1 tablespoon vanilla sugar*
- *90g (3oz) unsalted butter*
- *2–3 tablespoons chilled water*

Filling: *125g (4oz) marzipan*
- *4 eggs*
- *1/2 cup (110g/3 1/2oz) vanilla sugar*
- *1/3 cup (50g/2oz) plain flour*
- *1 tablespoon butter, melted*
- *1 1/4 cups (100g/3 1/2 oz) flaked almonds*
- *Icing sugar, to dust*

To make pastry, combine almond meal, flour and sugar in a bowl. Rub in butter until mixture resembles coarse breadcrumbs. Stir in chilled water until mixture clings together. With your fingers, work pastry into a ball, wrap in plastic wrap (film) and refrigerate for 20 minutes.

Preheat oven to 200°C/400°F/Gas Mark 5. Roll out pastry to fit a 23cm (9in) round or square flan tin with removable base. Trim edges, prick base with a fork, then place in freezer for 5 minutes.

MARZIPAN

When rolling marzipan, use icing sugar to dust the work surface. Marzipan should be stored at room temperature.

Line flan with baking paper, fill with rice or dried beans and bake blind for 12 minutes. Remove paper and weights. Reduce oven heat to 190°C/375°F/ Gas Mark 4. Return flan to oven and bake until base is dry. Remove from oven and reduce temperature to 170°C/340°F/Gas Mark 3.

Meanwhile, prepare filling. Roll out marzipan to fit base of flan; press into hot flan (you will probably need to patch it). Whisk eggs and sugar until pale and fluffy. Stir in flour and butter. Pour into flan and top with flaked almonds. Return to oven and bake for 20 minutes, or until filling is firm and top golden. Serve warm or at room temperature, dusted with icing sugar.

Spiced Coffee

Add thin strips of orange rind and a pinch of ground cloves to strongly brewed coffee. Pass dark brown sugar and a jug of hot or frothed milk. Provide cinnamon sticks to stir the coffee.

VEGETARIAN LUNCHEON

SERVES SIX

KUMARA PIKELETS WITH CHÈVRE AND ROASTED WALNUTS

- 2 kumara (orange sweet potato), about 750g (1½lb) before cooking
- ½ cup (125ml/4fl oz) milk
- 4 eggs
- 60g (2oz) butter, melted
- ¼ cup (60g/2oz) shaved palm sugar (or brown sugar)
- ½ cup (75g/2½oz) self-raising flour
- 1 teaspoon ground cardamom
- 1 teaspoon sea salt
- ⅔ cup (100g/3½oz) walnut pieces, roasted
- 200g (6½oz) soft chèvre
- ½ cup (125ml/4fl oz) walnut oil

Preheat oven to 150°C/300°F/Gas Mark 2. Wash kumara, trim ends, wrap in foil and roast for 1 hour, or until soft. Cool until easy to handle, then peel. Blend about 600g (19oz) of the flesh with the milk and eggs. Add butter, sugar, flour, cardamom and salt; blend until smooth.

Heat a griddle or heavy-based frying pan until a drop of water sizzles on the surface. Grease lightly with butter, then pour tablespoonfuls of mixture onto hot surface. Cook until bubbles appear in top of pikelets, flip over and cook other side. Remove and keep warm.

Grease surface between each batch. You may need to adjust temperature to keep heat even. These are quite soft pikelets. Serve with walnuts, chèvre, oil and freshly ground black pepper on the side.
Makes about 24.

MUSHROOM AND GREEN PEA RISOTTO

- 40g (1 ½ oz) dried sliced mushrooms
- 4 cups (1 L/3 2 fl oz) vegetable stock
- 1 tablespoon olive oil
- 1 tablespoon butter
- 1 small onion, finely diced
- 1 ½ cups (300g/9½oz) arborio rice
- 250g (8oz) sliced fresh pine or shiitake mushrooms
- 500g (1lb) frozen peas, thawed, or fresh peas, steamed
- 30g (1oz) butter, at room temperature, extra
- ½ cup chopped Italian (flat-leaf) parsley
- Shaved parmesan, to serve

Combine dried mushrooms and stock in a deep saucepan. Heat until simmering, remove from heat and stand for 10 minutes. Reheat and keep barely simmering.

Heat olive oil and butter in a heavy frying pan or paella pan. Add onion and rice and stir over medium heat until onion is translucent and rice is coated with oil. Stir in fresh mushrooms.

Place simmering stock next to frying pan on top of stove. Using a ladle, add quantities of simmering stock to rice, about ½ cup (125ml/4fl oz) at a time, stirring over medium heat until absorbed before adding more. Continue to add stock in this way until all has been used. Continue to cook risotto, stirring, until all liquid is absorbed. Rice grains should be tender, separated, creamy but not gluggy. Add peas and extra butter and stir until butter has melted and rice is glossy. Season to taste with salt and freshly ground black pepper. Serve, sprinkled with parsley. Pass shaved parmesan separately.

Opposite: Kumara Pikelets with Chèvre and Roasted Walnuts.

STICKY PLUM TART WITH NUTMEG AND GINGER

PASTRY: 1 ½ cups (225g/7oz) unbleached plain flour
- 1 tablespoon brown sugar
- 90g (3oz) unsalted butter, diced

FILLING: 1 kg (2lb) large, firm, ripe Autumn Giant plums, halved or quartered and stoned
- Finely julienned rind of 1 lemon
- 3 tablespoons brown sugar
- ½ teaspoon freshly grated nutmeg
- 2 teaspoons ground ginger
- 60g (2oz) unsalted butter, cut into 1cm (½in) pieces
- Cream, to serve

To make pastry, combine flour and sugar in a bowl. Rub in butter and add about 3 tablespoons chilled water until dough clings together. Shape into a flat disc, wrap in plastic wrap (film) and refrigerate for 20 minutes.

Preheat oven to 200°C/400°F/Gas Mark 5. Roll out pastry to fit a 23cm (9in) round or square flan tin with removable base. Trim edges and prick base with a fork. Place in freezer for 5 minutes. Line with baking paper and fill shell with baking weights, dried beans or rice. Bake for 10 minutes, remove from oven, remove paper and weights, pile in combined filling ingredients, except cream, and return to oven. Reduce temperature to 180°C/350°F/Gas Mark 4 and bake for 40 minutes, or until plums are soft and sticky. Serve warm with cream.

PICNIC LUNCH
AT THE RACES

| SERVES EIGHT

MARINATED ROASTED PORK FILLET
- *1 tablespoon mustard seed oil or peanut oil*
- *2kg (4lb) pork fillets (about 4 fillets)*

MARINADE: *¹/₃ cup (100g/3¹/₂oz) palm sugar, grated*
- *Finely grated rind and juice of 4–6 limes*
- *1 red chilli, seeded and chopped*

Combine marinade ingredients in a shallow dish. Add fillets and marinate for at least 1 hour. Preheat oven to 220°C/450°F/Gas Mark 6. Heat a frying pan until very hot, add oil and brown fillets quickly on all sides. Remove from pan. Roll fillets in marinade again, then transfer to a rack placed over a baking dish (reserve marinade for salad dressing). Pour a little water into the dish to prevent marinade from burning onto base. Roast in oven for 15 minutes, then allow to stand at room temperature for 10 minutes before slicing. Place in a covered dish to carry to picnic site.

...

CRISP DAIKON, WHITE CABBAGE AND NOODLE SALAD
- *1 daikon (white radish), peeled and julienned*
- *1 bulb fennel, sliced thinly*
- *Juice of 1 lemon*
- *4 green (spring) onions, sliced thinly on the diagonal*
- *3 sticks celery, julienned*
- *¹/₂ white cabbage, sliced thinly*
- *2 x 100g (3¹/₂oz packages pre-fried noodles)*

SWEET RICE WINE DRESSING:
- *³/₄ cup (190ml/6fl oz) reserved pork marinade*
- *¹/₂ cup (125ml/4fl oz) rice vinegar*
- *¹/₂ cup (125ml/4fl oz) sesame oil*

Opposite: Marinated Roasted Pork Fillet and Crisp Daikon, White Cabbage and Noodle Salad.

Make dressing first. Boil reserved marinade in a small saucepan for 2 minutes. Add vinegar and oil and pour into a jar, then seal. Combine salad vegetables in a large bowl with lemon juice. To serve, stir in noodles and dressing.

...

BRANDY AND PRUNE CAKE WITH THICK CREAM
- *500g (1lb) pitted prunes*
- *2 cups (500ml/16fl oz) brandy*
- *250g (8oz) unsalted butter, at room temperature*
- *1 cup (220g/7oz) caster sugar*
- *1 teaspoon vanilla essence*
- *4 eggs*
- *1²/₃ cup (250g/8oz) plain flour*
- *1 teaspoon baking powder*
- *Icing sugar, to serve*
- *Thick cream, to serve*

Combine prunes and brandy and stand for several hours. Preheat oven to 160°C/325°F/Gas Mark 3. Lightly grease a 23cm (9in) round or square springform tin and line base with baking paper. Cream butter, sugar and vanilla until pale and fluffy. Add eggs, 1 at a time, beating well after each addition. Fold in sifted flour and baking powder, then stir in prunes and brandy. Spoon into prepared tin. Bake for 1 hour. Cool in tin, then remove. Dust thickly with icing sugar and serve with thick cream.

BLACK GENOA FIGS AND BLACK MUSCAT GRAPES WITH TOMME FRAÎCHE
Buy firm ripe figs, unblemished grapes and a generous piece of tomme fraîche. Serve on a platter, with crackers or water biscuits.

TAKING-IT-EASY LUNCH

| SERVES SIX

STEAMED PRAWNS IN A BASKET WITH LEMONGRASS

- *2kg (4lb) king green prawns, washed and deveined*
- *Green tops of lemongrass*
(or cumin leaves or ginger leaves, optional)

CHILLI AND ZA'ATAR YOGHURT:
- *1 cup (250ml/8fl oz) natural plain yoghurt*
- *2 tablespoons za'atar (see Za'atar, p.58)*
- *1 large red chilli, seeded and chopped*

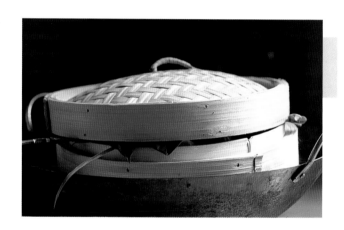

GINGER LEAVES AND CUMIN

Plant any pieces of unused ginger root (green ginger) in the garden or a pot. They will shoot to produce aromatic leaves that can then be used in the same way as lemongrass. Cumin plants are available at nurseries.

*Opposite: Steamed Prawns
in a Basket with Lemongrass.*

Make yoghurt mixture first. Combine ingredients in a serving bowl. Stand at room temperature for 30 minutes to allow flavours to develop. For prawns, place lemongrass or other leaves in base of a 30cm (12in) bamboo steamer basket. Lay prawns on top, cover with steamer lid and place over simmering water for 15–20 minutes, or until all prawns are orange. (If prawns are tightly packed, rearrange them during cooking to allow steam to reach each one.) Place basket on a serving plate and take to the table while prawns are hot. Provide a bowl for shells, and finger bowls and napkins for diners. Pass yoghurt mixture separately, for dipping.

PUMPKIN SOUP WITH CUMIN AND CRISP ONION GARNISH

- *1/4 cup (60ml/2fl oz) canola oil*
- *1 white stalk of lemongrass, finely chopped*
- *2.5cm (1in) piece fresh ginger root, finely chopped*
- *1 butternut pumpkin (about 1.5kg/3lb)*
- *4 cups (1L/32fl oz) chicken stock*

CRISP ONION GARNISH: *1kg (2lb) sweet yellow onions*
- *2 tablespoons canola oil*
- *1 tablespoon palm or brown sugar*

For soup, heat a large, heavy-based pan. Add oil, then lemongrass and ginger. Cover, reduce heat to lowest possible temperature. Cook, stirring occasionally, for 20–30 minutes, while preparing pumpkin and onion. Cut pumpkin into chunks, remove seeds and peel. Cut flesh into 5cm (2in) pieces, add to lemongrass and ginger in pot. Cover, increase heat to medium and cook, stirring occasionally, for 30 minutes. Add stock, bring to boil and simmer for 20 minutes. Blend until smooth (it is easier to use a blending wand in the cooking pan than to transfer mixture to a blender and back into pan). Reheat soup to serve.

For crisp onion garnish, peel onions and slice as thinly as possible. Heat a non-stick or heavy-based frying pan. Add oil, then onions. Cover tightly, reduce heat to lowest possible temperature. Cook, stirring very occasionally (the idea is to contain the steam as much as possible), for about 1 hour, or longer, while soup is cooking. About 15 minutes before serving, stir in palm sugar, and continue to cook onion, uncovered, for remaining time. Pass onion separately, in a bowl, to accompany soup, along with chunks of crusty bread.

MILE-HIGH APPLE PIE WITH BROWN SUGAR PASTRY

PASTRY: *3 cups (450g/14 1/2oz) plain flour*
- *2 tablespoons brown sugar*
- *1 teaspoon ground cinnamon*
- *90g (3oz) unsalted butter*
- *2 eggs, whisked with 1/2 cup (125ml/4fl oz) cold water*
- *1 tablespoon brown sugar, extra*

FILLING: *8 small Granny Smith apples, peeled and cut into thin wedges*
- *Juice of 1 lemon*
- *1 cup (200g/6 1/2oz) brown sugar*
- *1 teaspoon ground cinnamon*
- *60g (2oz) unsalted butter, cut into small cubes*
- *Pouring cream, to serve*

Combine filling ingredients, except butter and cream, in a bowl.

To make pastry, combine dry ingredients and rub in butter. Stir in egg and water with your hands. Work into a ball, wrap in baking paper and refrigerate for 20 minutes. Divide pastry in half. Roll out first piece between 2 sheets of baking paper to fit a 23cm (9in) pie dish. Peel off top paper and lift pastry on bottom piece. Invert pastry into pie dish, peel off paper. Re-use paper to roll out remaining pastry for lid.

Preheat oven to 170°C/340°F/Gas Mark 3.

Pile apple filling into pie dish, dot with butter, then position remaining pastry over top. Trim edges (reserve scraps for decoration) and press together gently to seal. Make a decorative pattern around the edge using the tines of a fork or your fingers. With a small sharp knife, make 4 x 6mm (1/4in) cuts in top of pie (to allow steam to escape). Sprinkle pie with extra brown sugar. Re-roll scraps of pastry and cut out decorative shapes. Press gently onto top of pie, over the sugar. Bake in centre of oven for 45 minutes, or until golden. If your oven has the facility, cook for the last 15 minutes with only the lower element on. Leave in turned-off oven until required. Serve with pouring cream.

AFTERNOON TEA FOR MUM

SHORT ALMOND BISCUITS

- *125g (4oz) unsalted butter, at room temperature*
- *1 cup (220g/7oz) caster sugar*
- *1 egg*
- *½ teaspoon vanilla essence*
- *1 tablespoon amaretto liqueur (or 1 teaspoon almond essence)*
- *1¾ cups (260g/8oz) self-raising flour*
- *½ cup (60g/2oz) ground almonds*
- *2 tablespoons milk*

Cream butter and sugar until pale and fluffy. Add egg, vanilla and amaretto and blend thoroughly. Combine flour and almonds. Add to butter mixture, a little at a time, alternating with milk and beating thoroughly after each addition.

Divide dough in half, shape into flat discs, wrap in plastic wrap (film) and refrigerate for 1 hour. Preheat oven to 190°C/375°F/Gas Mark 4. Line flat baking trays with baking paper. Roll out dough on a lightly floured surface to 3mm (⅛in) thickness. Using a shaped cutter of your choice, cut out 5–8cm (2–3in) cookies. Re-roll scraps to use all dough. Place on trays at least 1cm (½in) apart. Bake for 8–10 minutes, or until golden but not browned. Transfer to wire racks to cool. Store in an airtight container. (These cookies freeze well, as does the uncooked dough, which should be thawed in the refrigerator before using.) To serve, spread with Lemon Curd Spread (recipe follows).

. . .

LEMON CURD SPREAD

- *4 egg yolks*
- *¼ cup (55g/2oz) caster sugar*
- *Finely grated rind of 1 lemon*
- *1 cup (250ml/8fl oz) lemon juice*

Whisk egg yolks and sugar in top of a double boiler, or in a bowl placed over a saucepan of simmering water, until pale and aerated. Whisk in rind and juice and stir mixture over simmering water for about 10 minutes, or until thickened. Do not boil or mixture will curdle. If this happens, whisk another yolk in a clean bowl and slowly whisk curdled mixture into it.
Makes 1½ cups (375ml/12fl oz).

TINY CHOCOLATE PRUNE TARTS

PASTRY: *1/2 cup (80g/2 1/2oz) pure icing sugar*
• *125g (4oz) unsalted butter, at room temperature*
• *1 cup (150g/5oz) plain flour*
FILLING: *100g (3 1/2oz) bitter dark chocolate*
• *12–14 pitted dessert prunes*

Preheat oven to 150°C/300°F/Gas Mark 2.

Lightly spray a tray of tiny muffin cups with oil.
In an electric cake mixer or food processor, combine pastry ingredients and beat or process to a fine mealy texture. Squeeze mixture together with your fingers into a ball. Pinch off walnut-size pieces of pastry, roll into balls and place one in each muffin tin. Press down in centre of each with your thumb, to give an indent for filling and push mixture up sides.

Refrigerate for 5 minutes.

Break off a small piece of chocolate (about 7g/1/4oz) and stuff into each prune, closing prune around it. Remove muffin tray from refrigerator, place a prune in each pastry case and bake for 25–30 minutes, or until pastry is pale gold. Cool in tin to room temperature before removing (the pastry is delicate and will break if removed while warm).

Makes 12–14.

Opposite: Sponge Cake with Cinnamon Cream and Red Plum Purée.

SPONGE CAKE WITH CINNAMON CREAM AND RED PLUM PURÉE

• *3 large eggs, at room temperature*
• *1/2 cup (110g/3 1/2oz) caster sugar*
• *1/4 cup (35g/1oz) cornflour*
• *1/4 cup (35g/1oz) plain flour*
• *1/4 cup (35g/1oz) self-raising flour*
• *Icing sugar, for dusting*
FILLING: *1 1/4 cups (300ml/10 fl oz) double cream*
• *1 teaspoon ground cinnamon*

Preheat oven to 180°C/350°F/Gas Mark 4 with shelf positioned in centre. Lightly grease 2 deep, round 18cm (7in) cake tins. Line bases with greased baking paper. Sprinkle a teaspoon of flour into each tin, tap it around to barely coat sides; shake out any excess.

Beat eggs with electric mixer on medium–high speed for 7–10 minutes, or until pale and thick. Continue beating and add sugar, 1 tablespoon at a time, beating for another 3–5 minutes, or until sugar dissolves (mixture will feel smooth without any obvious grainy texture).

Sift flours together 3 times (to aerate), then sift again into egg mixture. Using a large metal spoon, carefully fold flour into egg, making sure it is completely incorporated, but do not overmix or the sponge will be tough. Pour into prepared tins and bake for 15–20 minutes, or until sponge is beginning to pull away from sides of tin and top feels springy to a light touch. Remove from oven, turn out of tin and cool, base-down, on a wire rack.

When ready to serve, place 1 cake on a serving plate. Lightly whip cream and cinnamon and pour about half onto the cake. Place second cake on top and dust with icing sugar. Pass plum purée (recipe follows) and remaining cream separately.

RED PLUM PURÉE: Place 6 large blood plums or late Autumn Giant plums, quartered and stones removed, in a saucepan with 1 tablespoon lemon juice, 1/2 teaspoon vanilla essence, 1/4 cup (55g/2oz) raw sugar and 1/4 teaspoon mixed spice. Cover and cook over lowest possible heat for 20 minutes. Remove from heat, cool uncovered, then process until smooth.

PÉTANQUE AND TEA AMONG THE LEAVES

| SERVES SIX

APPLE WEDGES TO DIP IN WARM CHEESE AND BEER SAUCE

- 3 each Golden Delicious and Pink Lady apples
- Juice of 1 lemon
- Crusty bread, cut into chunks

WARM CHEESE AND BEER SAUCE: 500g (1 lb) mixed shredded cheese (cheddar, mozzarella, parmesan)
- 2 tablespoons cornflour
- 1/2 teaspoon paprika
- 1 1/2 cups (375ml/12fl oz) beer, at room temperature

For sauce, combine cheese, cornflour and paprika in a bowl. Heat beer in a saucepan until beginning to simmer, then gradually stir in cheese mixture. Continue to stir until completely melted and smooth. Transfer to a pre-warmed wide-necked vacuum flask (preferably with a stainless-steel liner).

Cut apples into wedges and place in carrying container with lemon juice. Pack bread in another container and provide skewers for dipping tools. The sauce thickens as it cools, so a spreader knife is also useful.

Opposite: Apple Wedges and Warm Cheese and Beer Sauce.

PISTACHIO AND LEMON HONEY BAKLAVA

- 2 cups (300g/9 1/2oz) shelled pistachios
- 1/2 teaspoon cardamom seeds
- Thinly peeled rind of 1 lemon
- 12 sheets filo pastry
- 125g (4oz) butter, melted

SYRUP: 1/2 cup (125ml/4fl oz) honey
- 1/4 cup (60ml/2fl oz) lemon juice
- 2 tablespoon orange flower water

To make filling, boil syrup ingredients in a small saucepan with 1/4 cup (60ml/2fl oz) water for 3 minutes. Process pistachios, cardamom and lemon rind in a food processor or blender. Transfer to a bowl and stir in 1/3 cup (80ml/2 1/2fl oz) prepared syrup.

Preheat oven to 180°C/350°F/Gas Mark 4.

Lay filo on work surface. Brush top sheet with melted butter. Fold in thirds lengthways. Place a heaped tablespoonful of nut mixture on top right corner of pastry. Fold top left corner diagonally down over this to cover filling. Brush top with melted butter. Continue to fold pastry toward you in this way, to make a neat triangle, brushing top with butter after each fold. Continue with remaining pastry and filling, to make 12 triangles.

Pack closely together in a deep, lightly buttered 20 x 30cm (8 x 12in) baking dish. Bake baklava for 25 minutes, or until crisp and golden. Reheat syrup. Remove baklava from oven and immediately pour hot syrup over top to drench (it will bubble up around baklava). Cool in dish. (It is best to transport baklava in baking dish and serve directly from it.)

Makes 12 pieces.

LAMB SHANKS WITH GUINNESS

- 4–6 (about 2kg/4lb) lamb shanks
- ½ cup (75g/2½oz) plain flour
- ¼ cup (60ml/2fl oz) olive oil
- 3 large red onions, thinly sliced
- 2 bunches mint
- 3 cloves garlic, peeled and halved
- 2 cups (500ml/16fl oz) veal stock
- 3 cups (750ml/24fl oz) Guinness

Preheat oven to 160°C/325°F/Gas Mark 3. Place shanks in a large plastic bag, add flour and season to taste with salt and freshly ground black pepper. Holding bag closed, shake it to coat shanks with flour and seasonings. Heat oil to smoking point in a large, heavy-based ovenproof pot. Brown shanks, in batches, for about 5 minutes. Remove from pan. Spread onion over base of pot and mint leaves and garlic over onion. Put shanks on top, pour stock and Guinness into pot, cover and cook in oven for 3 hours. Remove lid, turn shanks and cook for 30 minutes more. Remove shanks from pot, cover and keep warm.
Strain cooking liquid into a clean saucepan, discarding solids. Simmer over high heat until reduced to about 2 cups (500ml/16fl oz). Season to taste. Serve shanks with hot sauce and Parmesan Polenta (recipe follows).

PARMESAN POLENTA

- 2 cups (500ml/16fl oz) veal or chicken stock
- 2 cups (500ml/16fl oz) milk
- 60g (2oz) butter
- 1½ cups (250g/8oz) polenta (cornmeal)
- ¼ cup (20g/⅔oz) grated parmesan
- 1 cup chopped parsley

In a deep saucepan, heat stock and milk until simmering. Add butter and stir, in one direction, with the handle of a large wooden spoon, to create a vortex in the liquid.

Continue stirring and pour in polenta in a slow, steady stream. (The movement of the liquid helps to stop polenta from becoming lumpy.) Reduce heat to low and cook polenta, stirring, for 5 minutes. Cover and cook over the lowest possible heat, stirring occasionally for a further 10–15 minutes. Stir in parmesan and parsley and serve hot.

STICKY CARAMELISED APPLES ON BRIOCHE WITH CLOVE-SCENTED CREAM

- Juice and finely grated rind of ½ lemon
- 6 Golden Delicious apples
- 90g (3oz) butter
- ½ cup (100g/3½oz) brown sugar
- 1 egg
- ½ cup (125ml/4fl oz) milk
- 1 tablespoon caster sugar
- 4–6 slices sweet brioche, cut into star, diamond or other decorative shapes
- 1¼ cups (300ml/10fl oz) thick cream, to serve
- ½ teaspoon ground cloves, to serve

Place lemon juice and rind in a medium bowl. Peel, quarter and core apples, then cut each quarter in half again, retaining the wedge shape. Combine with lemon. Melt butter in a deep frying pan over low heat. Stir in brown sugar until dissolved. Increase heat, add apples and lemon, simmer for 10 minutes, stirring occasionally. Apples must be soft but retain their shape. Turn off heat and leave apples until required. Immediately before serving, remove apples with a slotted spoon to a warmed dish. Whisk egg, milk and sugar in a bowl. Heat caramel (apple cooking mixture) over medium heat until bubbling.
Dip brioche shapes in egg mixture and fry in the caramel for 1–2 minutes on each side, or until dark golden. Keep warm, with apples.
To serve, spoon apples onto warmed plates, top with brioche and pass cream with cloves stirred through, separately in a bowl.

LIGHT SUPPER
AFTER THE OPERA

| SERVES SIX

TINY TOFFEE FLORENTINES

- *1 1/4 cups (100g/3 1/2oz) flaked almonds, roasted until golden*
- *1/2 cup (100g/3 1/2oz) mixed peel*
- *1/3 cup (80g/2 1/2oz) mixed glacé fruit (ginger, peach, quince, apricot), finely diced*
- *90g (3oz) unsalted butter, diced*
- *1 cup (220g/7oz) caster sugar*
- *1/2 cup (125ml/4fl oz) water*
- *75g (2 1/2oz) dark cooking chocolate*

Lightly butter 3 flat baking trays. Have all ingredients ready. Combine almonds, peel and glacé fruit in a bowl. In a deep saucepan, combine butter, sugar and water. Stir over medium heat until butter dissolves and sugar has melted. Increase heat and boil until mixture starts to turn dark brown. Do not stir at all during this second stage. Watch carefully as mixture changes colour and remove from heat before it becomes too dark and begins to burn. Place saucepan on a board on the work surface and immediately add the nut and fruit mixture to the toffee, in one lot, stirring 2 or 3 times quickly to mix in. Too much stirring will make the toffee sugary. Have 2 teaspoons ready and using one to pick up mixture and the other to push it off the spoon, place little piles onto prepared trays.

You need to work quickly before the toffee sets. Each florentine will take on its own irregular shape. Leave on trays until set hard.
Melt chocolate in a bowl over simmering water or in a microwave oven. Place florentines, flat-base-up, on a wire rack over the sink. With a small metal spatula, spread chocolate on the base of each florentine and leave to set. Excess chocolate drips into the sink and is easy to clean up. Store florentines in an airtight container.
Makes about 28.

FRUIT AND CHEESE PLATTER

On a platter or serving board, arrange fresh Beurre Bosc pears and a sharp knife, walnuts in the shell with nutcrackers, a chunk of parmigiano reggiano and a cheese knife, cheese wafer biscuits and fresh dates.

THE BREAD

The bread in this menu can be made in advance and frozen, then thawed at room temperature the day you want to use it. Putting the bread in a plastic bag accelerates the rising process. If you don't have small bread tins, roll the dough into snakes 25cm (10in) long, roll in cornmeal and place directly on a baking tray.

WALNUT AND LEMON BREAD WITH FRESH OYSTERS

- ½ cup (125ml/4fl oz) lukewarm water
- 1 tablespoon brown sugar
- 7g (¼oz) sachet dry yeast
- 1½ cups (225g/7oz) unbleached plain flour
- 1 teaspoon salt
- 1 tablespoon butter, at room temperature
- ½ cup (60g/2oz) chopped walnuts
- Freshly grated rind of 1 lemon
- 2 teaspoons polenta (cornmeal)
- 36 fresh oysters
- Lemon wedges, to serve

Combine water with sugar and yeast in a small bowl. Stand 10 minutes, until foamy. Combine flour, salt and butter and work with your fingers until crumbly. Add walnuts and rind and then yeast mixture. Knead for 10 minutes, adding a teaspoon of extra water, if necessary, to achieve a dough of 'earlobe' texture. Lightly spray the inside of a large, clean plastic bag with oil (or drop a teaspoon of oil into bag and rub to coat inside). Knead dough into a ball, place in bag and tie top. Do not deflate bag when tying, as dough will emit gases that will inflate the bag. Place on a ceramic plate or bowl and stand in a warm draft-free place for 45 minutes, or until doubled in bulk. Spray 2 baking tins, each 25 x 5cm (10 x 2in) with oil, then sprinkle with polenta. Cut dough in half. Knead into snake shapes, 25cm (10in) long. Place in tins. Sprinkle top with polenta. Cover with plastic (or put tins in plastic bag, as before). Leave to rise as before for a further 30 minutes. Preheat oven to 200°C/400°F/Gas Mark 5. Bake bread for 10–15 minutes, or until well-risen and lightly brown. Turn out and stand for at least 30 minutes before using. Serve, sliced, on a platter with fresh oysters and lemon wedges. Provide little wooden skewers for oysters and a bowl for the empty shells.

Opposite: Walnut and Lemon Bread with Fresh Oysters.

Sweet endings for Late Supper

COFFEE CREAM CAKE

- *125g (4oz) unsalted butter, at room temperature*
- *1 cup (220g/7oz) caster sugar*
- *2 eggs*
- *⅔ cup (160ml/5 fl oz) milk*
- *2 tablespoons coffee essence*
- *2 cups (300g/9½oz) self-raising flour, sieved*
- *½ cup (60g/2oz) finely chopped walnuts*

COFFEE CREAM:
- *1¼ cups (300ml/10 fl oz) thickened cream*
- *1 teaspoon coffee essence*
- *2 teaspoons icing sugar*
- *3 tablespoons drinking chocolate*
- *1 tablespoon Tia Maria (optional)*

Preheat oven to 180°C/350°F/Gas Mark 4. Lightly grease 2 x 18cm (7in) springform tins with butter, and line bases with baking paper. Cream butter and sugar until pale and fluffy. Add eggs, one at a time, beating well after each addition. Mix in combined milk and coffee essence, then gradually add flour and walnuts. Pour mixture into prepared tins and bake for 30 minutes, or until cakes test done. Cool in tins for 5 minutes, then transfer to a wire rack. When cakes are completely cold, beat coffee cream ingredients together until thick. Place 1 cake on a serving plate, spread top with half the cream and place second cake on top. Spread this with remaining cream. This cake keeps well, covered, in the refrigerator, for several days.

Opposite: Pear Galette.

CHOCOLATE NUTS

Lightly roast about 2 cups (250g/8oz) mixed raw nuts. Melt 125g (4oz) dark cooking chocolate in a bowl. Drop nuts into chocolate; remove individually with a fork, letting excess chocolate drip back into container. Place chocolate-coated nuts on a tray lined with baking paper and leave to set. Re-melt chocolate, re-dip nuts, so that bottoms are also coated with chocolate. Place on tray. Serve in a small bowl.

...

PEAR GALETTE

- *2 sheets frozen pre-rolled puff pastry, thawed*
- *1 egg yolk, whisked with a fork*
- *3 firm, ripe Red D'Anjou or Sensation pears*
- *Juice of 1 lemon*
- *2 tablespoons brown sugar*
- *15g (½oz) butter*
- *Thick cream, to serve*

Preheat oven to 180°C/350°F/Gas Mark 4. Lightly grease a flat oven tray. Place 1 sheet of pastry on prepared tray. Brush with yolk and place second sheet on top. Using a sharp knife and a saucepan lid as a guide, cut as large a circle as possible from the pastry.

Cut pears, from stem to base, into 3mm (⅛in) slices, leaving stem and core intact. As you cut them, place slices on a plate and sprinkle with lemon juice to prevent discoloration. Sprinkle half the brown sugar over surface of pastry. Arrange pear slices, overlapping, in a circle, on top, leaving a clear margin 2.5cm (1in) around edge. Sprinkle remaining sugar over pears and dot with butter.

Pinch in edge of pastry to form a decorative ring. Bake for 20 minutes, or until pastry is puffed and golden. Slide onto serving plate. Serve warm with cream.

WINTER

BRUNCH
IN A COSY BED

CODDLED EGGS WITH
TUNA PASTE ON TOAST FINGERS
- *8 slices Turkish bread, each 1 cm (1/2 in) thick, toasted*
- *4 large eggs, at room temperature*
- *Caperberries, to serve, optional*

TUNA AND CAPER PASTE:
- *150–200g (5–6 1/2 oz) tuna, in a single piece*
- *1 tablespoon butter*
- *2 tablespoons tiny capers*
- *1 tablespoon mayonnaise*

LEMON BUTTER: *60g (2 oz) unsalted butter*
- *Finely grated rind of 1 lemon*

To make paste, place tuna, butter and capers on
a plate over a saucepan of simmering water. Cover
and cook for 15 minutes, or until done to your liking.
Transfer to a bowl, add mayonnaise and, using a fork,
mash to a coarse paste. Spread on toast slices
and cut into fingers.

To coddle eggs, bring 2 cups (500ml/16fl oz) water
to the boil in a saucepan, lower in eggs, turn off heat
and stand for 8–10 minutes. Remove eggs.
For lemon butter, melt butter with rind and coarsely
ground black pepper to taste. Pour into small warmed
dishes. Place on breakfast tray with toast and eggs.
Serve immediately. Provide a small knife and spoons
for the eggs. Toast fingers are dipped in
the hot lemon butter.

*Opposite: Coddled Eggs with
Tuna Paste on Toast Fingers.*

INDIVIDUAL BRIOCHE AND
MASCARPONE RHUBARB PUDDINGS
- *4 stalks rhubarb*
- *1/4 cup (60ml/2fl oz) orange juice*
- *3 slices sweet (yellow) brioche, about 1 cm (1/2 in) thick*
- *1/2 cup (125g/4oz) mascarpone*
- *1 egg*
- *1/2 cup (125ml/4fl oz) pouring cream*
- *1 tablespoon caster sugar*

Preheat oven to 180°C/350°F/Gas Mark 4.
Butter 2 ramekins or heatproof dishes, each about
1-cup (250ml/8fl oz) capacity. Combine rhubarb
and orange juice in a small non-reactive saucepan,
cover and simmer over low heat for 10 minutes.
Cool slightly. Spread both sides of brioche slices with
mascarpone. Layer brioche and rhubarb into prepared
ramekins, starting and finishing with brioche. Whisk
together egg, cream and sugar. Pour mixture over
brioche, letting it soak in. Bake for 15–20 minutes,
or until golden and slightly puffed. Serve hot.

BRIOCHE
Sweet yellow brioche is available from most supermarkets as a soft plaited loaf. Not to be confused
with the sugar-topped brioche from bakeries.

FRESH APPLE AND GRAPEFRUIT JUICE
Put Granny Smith apples and peeled ruby grapefruit
through a juice extractor, chill before serving (or buy
good-quality apple juice and combine with freshly
squeezed grapefruit juice).

BRUNCH GOING TO THE SNOW FIELDS

ARANCI

- *2 cups (400g/12½oz) arborio rice*
- *1 tablespoon finely chopped parsley*
- *¾ cup (60g/2oz) grated parmesan*
- *4 eggs, beaten lightly*
- *1 cup (150g/5oz) plain flour*
- *2 cups (200g/6½oz) packaged dry breadcrumbs*
- *Light olive oil, for deep-frying*

BEEF AND TOMATO FILLING: *1 tablespoon olive oil*
- *155g (5oz) minced (ground) beef*
- *2 cloves garlic*
- *400g (12½oz) canned peeled tomatoes*
- *¼ cup chopped basil*
- *¾ cup (75g/2½oz) grated mozzarella*

SPINACH AND RICOTTA FILLING:
- *1 bunch English spinach, washed and trimmed*
- *1 clove garlic, finely chopped*
- *1¼ cups (250g/8oz) fresh ricotta, drained*
- *1 egg, beaten*
- *¼ teaspoon freshly grated nutmeg*

Cook rice, stirring occasionally, in plenty of boiling salted water for 12 minutes. Drain in a colander, then spread on a clean tea towel to cool.

To make beef filling, heat oil in a frying pan. Brown beef over high heat. Add garlic and crushed tomatoes, with their juice. Simmer for about 5 minutes, or until liquid has evaporated. Remove from heat, stir in basil and season to taste with salt and black pepper. Cool, then stir in mozzarella. Set aside until required.

To make spinach filling, place spinach in a deep saucepan, add garlic, cover, and cook briefly over medium heat until wilted. Drain through a colander. When cold, chop roughly and combine with ricotta, egg and nutmeg. Set aside until required.

To shape aranci, combine rice in a large bowl with parsley, parmesan and ¼ cup (60ml/2fl oz) of the beaten egg.

Have flour, remaining egg and breadcrumbs ready in separate bowls on the work surface. Place a tray, lined with baking paper, ready to take finished aranci. Take a large spoonful of rice mixture and place in your cupped hand. With the back of the spoon, make a little hollow in centre of rice. Place a tablespoon of either filling in this hollow. Spoon a little more rice on top. With both hands, mould rice into a pear shape, entirely enclosing the filling. Dust with flour, dip in egg and coat with breadcrumbs. Place on tray and repeat with remaining ingredients. Aranci can be covered and refrigerated at this point, for frying later, or fried and reheated.

To fry, pour 10cm (4in) olive oil into a saucepan and heat to 170°C/340°F. Cook aranci in batches of 2, lowering them into the oil with a large slotted spoon. Turn frequently during cooking, until aranci are a deep golden brown. Adjust temperature of oil during cooking to prevent it from becoming too hot. (If it does, the aranci will split and the filling will spill out.) Remove with a slotted spoon and drain on paper towels; for transportation, wrap in napkins and foil.

Makes about 10.

Opposite: Aranci.

PRUNE, WALNUT AND MAPLE MUFFINS

- *3 eggs*
- *1 cup (250ml/8 fl oz) pouring cream*
- *⅔ cup (160ml/5 fl oz) pure maple syrup*
- *1½ cups (225g/7oz) self-raising flour*
- *1⅓ cups (125g/4oz) rolled oats*
- *1 tablespoon ground cinnamon*
- *1¼ cups (200g/6½oz) pitted dessert prunes, chopped*
- *1⅔ cups (200g/6½oz) walnut halves*

SPREAD: *¾ cup (200g/6½oz) cream cheese, at room temperature*
- *2 tablespoons pure maple syrup*
- *Finely grated rind of 1 lemon*

Preheat oven to 190°C/375°F/Gas Mark 4.
Line 2 trays of 12 large muffin cups with paper cases. Whisk eggs with cream and maple syrup (reserving 1 tablespoon syrup). Combine flour, oats and cinnamon in a bowl. Make a well in centre and pour in egg mixture. Stir just to combine. Stir in prunes. Reserve 20 walnut halves and chop remainder; stir chopped nuts into mixture. Spoon mixture into muffin cups to three-quarters fill. Top each with a walnut halve and drizzle with reserved maple syrup.
Bake for 20 minutes. Wrap in a clean tea towel and transport in a basket.
Beat spread ingredients together and pack in a separate container. Provide a small spreader knife.

Makes 20.

...

CAFÉ AU LAIT WITH DARK CHOCOLATE

Mix good-quality espresso with steaming-hot milk and pour into a pre-warmed vacuum flask.
Pack a block of the best dark chocolate you can find.
Break a stick and dip into your coffee, then suck the melted chocolate off. Smile!

BREAKFAST CALZONES

DOUGH: *1 teaspoon olive oil*
- *7g (¼oz) dried yeast*
- *125ml (½ cup/4 fl oz) lukewarm water*
- *2 cups (300g/9½oz) unbleached bread flour*
- *1 egg, beaten*
- *Light olive oil, for deep-frying*

FILLINGS: *90g (3oz) ham or hot sausage, chopped*
- *200g (6½oz) cooked potato, diced*
- *125g (4oz) corn kernels (canned or frozen)*
- *1 tablespoon capers*
- *90g (3oz) mozzarella, grated*

OR: *90g (3oz) mushrooms, thinly sliced*
- *250g (8oz) fresh ricotta*
- *1 teaspoon ground aniseed*
- *90g (3oz) grated parmesan*

To make dough, combine olive oil with a pinch of sea salt, the yeast and lukewarm water in a jug. Stand for 10 minutes, or until yeast dissolves and mixture looks creamy. Place flour in a mixing bowl, make a well in the centre and pour in yeast mixture. Stir to combine, then knead for 10 minutes. Shape into a ball. Lightly oil a ceramic bowl. Place dough in it, cover with plastic wrap (film) and then a clean tea towel. Stand in a warm, draft-free place for about 1 hour, or until tripled in bulk. Knock down, divide dough into 4 pieces, roll into oval shapes about 3mm (⅛in) thick. Brush tops and sides with beaten egg. Combine chosen filling ingredients. Spoon onto one (lengthways) half of the oval shape and fold other side over filling to cover. Seal edges by pinching together. Rest for 5 minutes. Heat oil in a large, deep pan to 170°C/340°F. Cook calzone in batches of 2. Deep-fry for 3–4 minutes, turning frequently. Remove and drain on paper towels. Adjust temperature of oil during cooking to prevent it from becoming too hot. Cool calzone to room temperature and wrap in napkins for transportation.

DOUGHNUTS ON A RAINY MORNING

| SERVES EIGHT

GLAZED ORANGE DOUGHNUTS

- *2 large oranges (use Sevilles for a bitter orange taste)*
- *1 large egg*
- *1 1/4 cups (300ml/10fl oz) sour cream*
- *1/3 cup (75g/2 1/2oz) caster sugar*
- *60g (2oz) unsalted butter, melted*
- *3 1/4 cups (485g/15 1/2oz) plain flour*
- *2 teaspoons baking powder*
- *1 teaspoon baking soda*
- *3/4 teaspoon salt*
- *8 cups (2L/64fl oz) vegetable oil*

GLAZE: *2 cups (320g/10oz) pure icing sugar, sifted*
- *Finely julienned rind of 2 oranges*
- *2/3 cup (160ml/5fl oz) strained orange juice*

Grate rind from 2 oranges into a large bowl.
Cut up oranges, discarding pith and seeds, and process in a blender to a pulp—yields about 1 cup (250ml/8fl oz). Add to rind with egg, sour cream, sugar and butter and mix well. Sift flour with baking powder, baking soda and salt. Stir into wet mixture until well combined, to give a soft dough.
Turn out on a well-floured surface and knead until smooth. Pat dough out to 1cm (1/2in) thickness.
Dip a 6cm (2 1/2in) doughnut cutter in flour and cut out doughnuts. Place doughnuts, and holes, on a tray lined with baking paper.
Re-roll any scraps and continue to cut out doughnuts until mixture is used. (Doughnuts can be covered and frozen at this stage. Thaw before frying.)
Heat oil in a large, deep saucepan to 170°C/340°F, or until a cube of bread, when dropped in, immediately

JULIENNED RIND

Use a citrus zester—a small tool with a metal head with a row of small holes—to create julienned rind. These are available from kitchenware shops.

---

bubbles to the surface and begins to brown. Use a slotted spoon to lower each doughnut into the oil, cooking 3 doughnuts and 3 holes in each batch. Cook for 2–3 minutes, turning doughnuts as they rise to the surface and 3 or 4 times more during cooking. Remove with a slotted spoon and place on a tray lined with absorbent paper to drain.
To make the thin glaze, mix icing sugar, julienned rind and orange juice in a large bowl. While doughnuts are warm, dip them in glaze and place on a wire rack over the sink. Let glaze set; pour any remaining glaze mixture over doughnuts. The drips will fall into the sink and can easily be washed away.
Makes 12.

GINGER PINEAPPLE DOUGHNUTS

- 60g (2oz) unsalted butter, melted
- 1/2 cup (110g/3 1/2oz) raw sugar
- 2 large eggs
- 1/2 cup (125ml/4fl oz) sour cream
- 1/4 cup drained, crushed pineapple
- 1/4 cup (30g/1oz) crystallised ginger, chopped
- 3 1/2 cups (525g/17oz) plain flour
- 1 teaspoon freshly grated nutmeg
- 1 teaspoon ground cinnamon
- 1 teaspoon ground ginger
- 2 teaspoons baking powder
- 1 teaspoon baking soda
- 1 teaspoon salt
- 8 cups (2L/64fl oz) vegetable oil
- 1 tablespoon ground cinnamon
- 2 tablespoons caster sugar

Beat melted butter in a large bowl with raw sugar, eggs, sour cream, pineapple and ginger. Sift flour with nutmeg, cinnamon, ginger, baking powder, baking soda and salt. Stir into wet mixture until just combined, to give a soft dough.

Turn out on a well-floured surface and knead lightly until smooth. Pat dough out to 1cm (1/2in) thickness. Dip a 6cm (2 1/2in) doughnut cutter in flour and cut out doughnuts. Place doughnuts, and holes, on a tray lined with baking paper. Re-roll any scraps and continue to cut out doughnuts until mixture is all used.

Heat oil in a large, deep saucepan to 170°C/340°F or until a cube of bread, when dropped in, immediately bubbles to the surface and begins to brown. Use a slotted spoon to lower each doughnut into the oil, cooking 3 doughnuts and 3 holes in each batch. Cook for 2–3 minutes, turning doughnuts as they rise to surface and 3 or 4 times more during cooking. Remove with a slotted spoon and place on a tray lined with absorbent paper to drain.

Combine cinnamon and caster sugar in a shaker or sieve. While doughnuts are still warm, sprinkle both sides liberally with cinnamon sugar.

Makes 10–12.

DOUGHNUTS

All these recipes are quick as there is no yeast involved. The orange doughnuts keep best and are quite acceptable the next day. The others should be eaten the same day.

COFFEE CHURROS

- 1/2 cup (125ml/4fl oz) milk
- 2 tablespoons sugar
- 125g (4oz) unsalted butter, at room temperature
- 1 cup (150g/5oz) plain flour, sifted
- 4 eggs, at room temperature
- 1 tablespoon coffee essence
- 8 cups (2L/64fl oz) vegetable oil
- 1 tablespoon ground cinnamon
- 2 tablespoons caster sugar

Place milk, sugar and butter in a deep, heavy-based saucepan and bring to a boil. When butter has melted, reduce heat to medium, add flour all together and beat with a wooden spoon for about 2 minutes, or until mixture is smooth and glossy and pulls away from sides of pan. Remove from heat. Beat in eggs, one at a time, beating well after each addition. Beat in coffee essence. Transfer mixture to a piping bag fitted with a 1cm (1/2in) star nozzle. Heat oil in a large, deep saucepan to 170°C/340°F, or until a cube of bread, when dropped in, immediately bubbles to the surface and begins to brown. Pipe 20cm (8in) lengths of dough into oil, cooking 3 or 4 churros in each batch. Cook for 2–3 minutes, turning churros as they rise to surface and 3 or 4 times more during cooking. Remove with a slotted spoon and place on a tray lined with absorbent paper to drain. Combine cinnamon and sugar in a shaker or sieve. While churros are still warm, sprinkle both sides liberally with cinnamon sugar.

Makes about 12.

Opposite: Coffee Churros, Ginger Pineapple Doughnuts and Glazed Orange Doughnuts.

MORNING TEA AT THE GAME

RICH RUM STICKY BUNS

- *7g (¹/₄oz) dry yeast*
- *2 tablespoons brown sugar*
- *2 tablespoons milk, warmed*
- *¹/₄ cup (60ml/2 fl oz) thick cream or sour cream*
- *¹/₂ teaspoon vanilla essence*
- *Finely grated rind of 1 lemon*
- *1 teaspoon lemon juice*
- *1 egg yolk*
- *1 ¹/₂ cups (225g/7oz) plain flour*
- *60g (2oz) butter*

FILLING: *¹/₂ teaspoon cinnamon*
- *¹/₃ cup (50g/1³/₄oz) currants*
- *3 tablespoons dark rum*
- *¹/₂ cup (100g/3¹/₂oz) dark brown sugar*
- *¹/₄ cup (60ml/2 fl oz) honey*

For dough, combine yeast, brown sugar, warm milk and a pinch of salt in a jug. Mix to dissolve yeast and stand for 10 minutes, or until mixture is creamy.
Combine with cream or sour cream, vanilla, lemon rind and juice in a mixing bowl, stirring until smooth.
Add egg yolk and half the flour and combine; beat in remaining flour and knead for 10 minutes, or until dough is of 'earlobe' texture. Shape into a ball.
Lightly spray the inside of a clean plastic bag with oil.
Place dough in bag and seal (do not squeeze out air).
Place on a ceramic plate in a warm, draft-free place for 1 hour, or until doubled in bulk.

STICKY BUNS
The dough for the rich rum sticky buns can be prepared the night before and left in the refrigerator overnight to rise slowly.

Combine cinnamon, currants and rum and soak while dough is rising. Preheat oven to 180°C/350°F/ Gas Mark 4. Place a small knob of butter in each of 18 tiny muffin cups. Place in a barely warm oven until melted; remove from oven. Combine brown sugar and honey in a small bowl and set aside.
Turn dough out on a lightly floured work surface and roll into a rectangle 30 x 10cm (12 x 4in).
Spread filling over rectangle, leaving a clear margin 1cm (¹/₂in) wide along both long edges. Fold in long sides to trap liquid, then roll in from each side to form a long log. (Some liquid will escape from ends. Use this to brush on buns once they are in the muffin cups.) Cut roll into 2cm (³/₄in) lengths.
Spoon 1 teaspoon of honey mixture into each cup.
Place slices of roll, cut-sides-up-and-down, in tins.
Brush tops with liquid from board. Bake for 15–20 minutes, or until risen and golden. Remove immediately from cups to a wire rack to cool.
(If buns stick in muffin cups, return briefly to the oven to re-soften bases).
Makes 18.

Opposite: Rich Rum Sticky Buns.

To peel tomatoes, cut out the core end with a sharp knife and score the base of each tomato with an X. Place in a pot of boiling water, return water to the boil, then scoop out with a slotted spoon. Place in cold water. The skins will peel off easily.

POTATO, LEEK AND HAM SOUP

- *1 tablespoon olive oil*
- *60g (2oz) butter*
- *2 leeks, white part only, washed and sliced*
- *1 kg (2lb) old potatoes, peeled and cut into 2cm (³/₄in) cubes*
- *1 small ham hock or 250g (8oz) ham pieces*
- *4 cups (1L/32fl oz) chicken stock*
- *¹/₂ cup (125ml/4fl oz) pouring cream*

Heat oil and butter in a heavy-based saucepan, add leek and potato and stir. Cover and cook, stirring occasionally, over medium heat for about 10 minutes.

Add ham and stock and enough water to cover ingredients in saucepan. Bring to a simmer and cook, uncovered, for 30 minutes. Remove hock or scoop out meat with a slotted spoon and set aside. Using a blending wand, blend soup in saucepan, or transfer to a blender, or pass through a coarse sieve. Stir in cream and reheat without boiling. Season to taste with freshly ground white pepper. Cut meat off hock and return to pan, or return ham pieces. Pour into 1 or 2 warmed vacuum flasks for transportation. Serve in mugs.

REAL TOMATO SOUP

- *1 tablespoon olive oil*
- *60g (2oz) butter*
- *2 large red onions, peeled and diced*
- *1 red chilli, seeded and chopped*
- *1 stick celery, chopped*
- *1 kg (2lb) ripe tomatoes, peeled and roughly chopped*
- *4 cups (1L/32fl oz) chicken stock*
- *1 cup chopped chervil, Italian (flat-leaf) parsley, or chives, or a mixture*

Heat olive oil and butter in a heavy-based saucepan, add onion, chilli and celery and cook, stirring occasionally, over low heat until onion is translucent. Add tomatoes and stir to combine. Add stock, bring to a simmer and cook, uncovered, for 30 minutes. Using a blending wand, blend soup in the saucepan, or transfer to a blender, or pass through a coarse sieve. Reheat, stir in herbs and season to taste with salt and black pepper. Pour into 1 or 2 warmed vacuum flasks for transportation. Serve in mugs.

LUNCH WITH INDIAN FLAVOURS

| SERVES SIX

PRAWN SAMOSAS

- *24 samosa wrappers*
- *Juice of 1 lime or lemon*
- *48 coriander (cilantro) leaves*
- *500g (1lb) royal red prawn meat (fresh, or frozen and thawed)*
- *Peanut oil, for shallow-frying*

Brush each samosa wrapper with juice, place
2 coriander leaves in centre and 2–3 prawns on top.
Fold wrapper around prawns and seal edges by
pinching together. Heat about 5cm (2in) oil
in a heavy-based saucepan. Fry samosas in batches.
(Do not crowd the pan.) Remove with a slotted
spoon and drain on absorbent paper.
Serve hot or warm, with drinks.

GHEE

Available from supermarkets, ghee is a type of clarified
butter. It has been simmered until all its moisture has
evaporated and the milk solids have just started to brown.
It has a high smoke point and is used extensively for
frying in Indian and Middle Eastern cooking.

GARLIC AND LEMON SPINACH

- *¹/₂ cup (125g/4oz) ghee or light vegetable oil*
- *6 whole cloves garlic, peeled*
- *Finely julienned rind of 1 lemon*
- *1 tablespoon turmeric*
- *2 bunches English spinach, washed, dried and tough stalks removed*

Melt ghee in a deep frying pan over low heat.
Add garlic, lemon rind and turmeric and cook, stirring,
for 5 minutes. Do not let garlic brown. Add spinach
and stir to coat with ghee. Cover and simmer for
5 minutes. Season to taste with salt and freshly
ground black pepper. Serve hot.

CARROTS WITH MUSTARD SEEDS

- *1 tablespoon yellow or brown mustard seeds*
- *½ cup (125ml/4fl oz) mustard seed oil*
- *2 tablespoons lime juice*
- *1 teaspoon sea salt*
- *3 cups grated raw carrot*

Place mustard seeds in a small saucepan, cover, and cook, shaking pan to prevent burning, over low heat until seeds begin to pop. Add mustard seed oil, lime juice, sea salt and freshly ground black pepper to taste. Heat until just starting to simmer. Place carrot in a bowl and pour mustard seed mixture over. Toss to coat well and serve at room temperature.

BONED LEG OF LAMB
WITH SPICED YOGHURT

- *2 cups (500g/1lb) plain natural yoghurt*
- *2 medium onions, peeled and quartered*
- *2.5cm (1in) piece fresh ginger root, peeled and chopped roughly*
- *1 cup (150g/5oz) raw almonds*
- *2 tablespoons ground coriander*
- *1 tablespoon ground cardamom*
- *1 teaspoon freshly ground black pepper*
- *1 tablespoon sea salt*
- *1 Ezy-cut (boned and re-rolled) leg of lamb (1.7–2kg/3½–4lb)*
- *4 large Desiree or Pontiac potatoes, washed and cut into 2.5cm (1in) cubes*

Preheat oven to 160°C/325°F/Gas Mark 3. Combine yoghurt, onion, ginger, almonds, coriander, cardamom, pepper and salt in a blender or food processor and process to a coarse paste. Place in a heavy, ovenproof casserole, add meat and turn to coat with the paste. Cover casserole and bake for 2½ hours. Add potatoes and cook for 1 hour more. (This can be made up to 2 days before and refrigerated, then gently reheated. If the sauce is still thick after heating, thin with a little cream or milk.) Cut meat into thick slices and serve with sauce and potatoes spooned on top, accompanied by Carrots with Mustard Seeds and Garlic and Lemon Spinach.

BAKED RICOTTA AND COCONUT
PUDDINGS WITH PAWPAW

- *¾ cup (45g/1½oz) desiccated coconut*
- *Butter, for greasing moulds*
- *½ pawpaw (papaya)*
- *⅓ cup (70g/2½oz) brown sugar*
- *750g (1½lb) fresh ricotta*
- *2 tablespoons self-raising flour*
- *⅓ cup (70g/2½oz) brown sugar (extra)*
- *½ teaspoon ground cardamom*

Soak coconut in 1 cup (250ml/8fl oz) hot water for 10 minutes. Preheat oven to 160°C/325°F/Gas Mark 3. Butter 6 individual ½-cup (125ml/4fl oz) moulds or ramekins. Slice pawpaw, place on a flat dish and sprinkle with brown sugar. Cover and refrigerate while preparing the puddings (sugar will melt). Drain coconut in a sieve, pressing out any excess water with the back of a spoon. Combine with remaining ingredients. Pour mixture into prepared moulds or ramekins. Bake, uncovered, for 45–60 minutes, or until tops are firm and lightly browned. Remove from oven, cool slightly. Loosen sides with a small metal spatula and turn out on serving plates. Serve with pawpaw and brown sugar syrup.

Opposite: Boned Leg of Lamb with Spiced Yoghurt, Carrots with Mustard Seeds, Garlic and Lemon Spinach.

LUNCH WITH BOUILLABAISSE

SERVES EIGHT

BOUILLABAISSE SERVED
WITH BREAD AND AÏOLI

FISH: *1 kg (2lb) green king prawns*
- *1 kg (2lb) mussels, washed under cold water
and beards removed*
- *1 kg (2lb) cockles (vongole), washed under cold water*
- *500g (1lb) red fish fillets, cut into large chunks*
- *500g (1lb) flathead fillets, cut into large chunks*
- *2 cups (500ml/16fl oz) white wine*

FISH STOCK: *1–2 fish heads (snapper, salmon)*
- *Prawn shells and heads*
- *1 cup (250ml/8fl oz) white wine*

BASE: *1 tablespoon olive oil*
- *1 leek, chopped*
- *1 onion, chopped*
- *2 cloves garlic, chopped*
- *1 bulb fennel, sliced*
- *1 kg (2lb) ripe tomatoes, peeled and chopped*
- *1 teaspoon saffron threads,
soaked in 2 tablespoons boiling water*
- *3 tablespoons tomato paste*
- *Small bunch fresh thyme*
- *2 fresh bay leaves*
- *Sliced Italian bread, to serve*
- *Aïoli, to serve (recipe follows)*

Peel prawns, leaving tails intact. Place heads and shells
in stock pot. Devein prawns, cover and refrigerate.
Prepare remaining seafood, cover and refrigerate.

Opposite: Bouillabaisse.

BOUILLABAISSE

The list of ingredients for bouillabaisse may look
daunting, but the base and aïoli can be prepared
in advance and refrigerated. The preparation
of the sauce takes time, not effort. There are no rules
about the fish you use—the dish was originally
devised to use the fishermen's catch, so a different
combination of fish was used each time. The main rule
of thumb is to add the seafood last and cook briefly.

To make stock, add fish heads to prawn shells, add
wine and 16 cups (4L/128fl oz) cold water. Bring to
the boil, reduce heat and simmer, partly covered, for
1 hour. Strain, discarding solids. Reserve 3 cups
(750ml/24fl oz) of the stock in a container for aïoli.
To prepare base, heat oil in a large pot and cook leek,
onion, garlic and fennel over low heat, stirring
occasionally, for 10 minutes. Add tomatoes, saffron
and liquid, tomato paste, herbs and salt and pepper
to taste. Bring to a simmer and add strained stock.
Simmer, partly covered, for 2 hours.
To cook fish, heat wine in a large pot, add prepared
mussels and cockles and cook, covered, for 2 minutes.
(Discard any that do not open.) Pour in prepared
base, heat to a simmer and layer prawns and fish on
top. Cover and simmer for 5 minutes, or until fish is
opaque. There is no need to stir at this stage; cooking
the fish on top prevents it from breaking up. To serve,
ladle seafood into a heated covered serving bowl and
soup into another. Provide warm soup plates. Place aïoli
in a serving bowl on a platter with the bread. Serve soup
separately with bread and aïoli, then serve the seafood.

AÏOLI

- 1 tablespoon olive oil
- 1 leek, chopped
- 1 carrot, chopped
- 500g (1lb) tomatoes, peeled and chopped
- 3 tablespoons tomato paste
- 1/2 teaspoon saffron threads,
soaked in 1 tablespoon boiling water
- 3 cups (750ml/24 fl oz) fish stock
(reserved from Base in previous recipe)
- 125g (4oz) strong white bread,
crusts removed and cubed
- 2–3 cloves garlic
- 1/2 teaspoon cayenne or Tabasco
- 1/4 cup (60g/2oz) mayonnaise

Heat olive oil in a deep saucepan and cook leek and carrot, stirring, over medium heat for 2–3 minutes. Add tomatoes, tomato paste, saffron and liquid and reserved stock. Cover and cook over low heat for 2 hours (covered for the first hour, uncovered for the second, to allow sauce to reduce and thicken). Stir occasionally. Place bread and garlic in a blender, process to crumbs; pour in vegetable mixture and blend to a smooth thick sauce. Season with cayenne and transfer to a bowl. Cool, then stir in mayonnaise.

. . .

PARMESAN WAFERS

- 3 cups (250g/4oz) grated parmesan (or pecorino)
- 1 tablespoon fresh thyme leaves

Preheat oven to 160°C/325°F/Gas Mark 3. Line a baking tray with baking paper. Combine parmesan and thyme. Make little piles of 1 tablespoonful of mixture, spaced 2.5cm (1in) apart, on trays. Bake for 10 minutes, or until beginning to crisp at edges. Lift wafers and paper off trays and cool on a wire rack until firm. Peel wafers off paper and store in an airtight container. Serve with drinks.
Makes 18.

LITTLE PECAN PIES

PASTRY: 150g (5oz) unsalted butter, at room temperature
- 1 2/3 cups (250g/8oz) plain flour
- 1 cup (160g/5oz) sifted pure icing sugar
- 2 egg yolks
- 30g (1oz) butter, extra, melted
- Icing sugar, to serve
FILLING: 60g (2oz) butter, melted
- 1/2 cup (100g/3 1/2oz) brown sugar
- 1/2 cup (125ml/4 fl oz) pure maple syrup
- 2 egg yolks
- 1 teaspoon vanilla
- 2 cups (250g/8oz) pecans, chopped

To make pastry, combine butter, flour and icing sugar and work to the texture of fine breadcrumbs. Stir in egg yolks to give a smooth dough and shape into a roll 20cm (8in) long. Wrap in baking paper and refrigerate for 15 minutes.
Whisk filling ingredients, except pecans, together; stir in nuts. Preheat oven to 180°C/350°F/Gas Mark 4. Brush 10 friand tins or small muffin cups, each about 1/2 cup (125ml/4 fl oz) capacity, with melted butter. Slice pastry dough into 10 equal portions. Flatten each into a circle and press into the friand tins or muffin cups. Spoon filling into each and bake for 40–45 minutes. Cool in tins; turn out when barely warm. Sprinkle with icing sugar and serve. Accompany with cream or vanilla ice-cream, if desired.
Makes 10.

LUNCH TO SLEEP AFTER

STUFFING OLIVES

If you don't have a cherry pipper, buy stuffed green olives. Drain, remove the pimento and combine it with the mashed anchovy, then stuff it back in the olive or simply buy prestuffed anchovy olives.

ANCHOVY-STUFFED GREEN OLIVES

- *250g (8oz) queen, or large, green olives*
- *45g (1 1/2 oz) flat anchovy fillets, in oil*

Using a cherry pipper, remove olive stones. Drain anchovy fillets, placing oil in a small serving bowl. Mash anchovies and stuff into olives. Place in reserved oil. Serve with drinks.

OSSO BUCCO

- *12 large pieces veal shank, cut for osso bucco*
- *1/2 cup (75g/2 1/2 oz) plain flour*
- *1/4 cup (60ml/2 fl oz) olive oil*
- *1 large onion, chopped*
- *2 fresh bay leaves*
- *1 small bunch fresh thyme*
- *1 cup (250ml/8 fl oz) white wine*
- *1 kg (2lb) ripe tomatoes, peeled and chopped*
- *4 cups (1 L/32 fl oz) veal (or chicken) stock*
- *1 tablespoon rich veal glacé*

In a large clean plastic bag, combine veal shank and flour seasoned with salt and freshly ground black pepper. Holding bag closed, shake it to coat meat. Heat oil in a large, heavy-based casserole and brown meat, in batches. Remove from pan.

Preheat oven to 160°C/325°F/Gas Mark 3.

Add a little more oil if pan is dry and gently cook onion until softened. Add bay leaves, thyme and wine. Simmer for 3 minutes; add tomatoes and stock. Bring to a simmer and stir in veal glacé. Add meat, pushing down into liquid. Cover pan, place in oven and cook for 2 hours. Serve meat in shallow bowls with poundies (recipe follows). Spoon juices over.

POUNDIES WITH CELERIAC
AND LEMON BUTTER

- *500g (1lb) old potatoes,*
peeled and halved or quartered
- *1 large celeriac, peeled and cut into*
same size pieces as potatoes
- *Juice and finely grated rind of 1 lemon*
- *125g (4oz) butter, at room temperature*
- *1 1/2 cups (375ml/12fl oz) milk*

Place potatoes, celeriac and lemon juice in a saucepan,
cover with cold water and bring to the boil. Reduce
heat and simmer until vegetables are fork tender.
Strain off water and place pan back on low heat for a
minute to dry off vegetables. Add 30g (1oz) butter
and 1/2 cup (125ml/4fl oz) milk and heat until butter
has melted. Meanwhile, heat remaining milk to almost
simmering. Beat remaining butter with lemon rind.
Mash vegetables until fluffy. Serve hot, spooned into
a mound on a plate with osso bucco. Make a well
in centre of mash, pour in a little hot milk and
add a knob of lemon butter.

ORANGE FRIANDS WITH
STAR ANISE SYRUP

- *1/2 cup (75g/2 1/2oz) plain flour*
- *1 1/2 cups (240g/8oz) pure icing sugar*
- *1 cup (125g/4oz) ground almond meal*
- *Finely grated rind of 2 oranges*
- *180g (6oz) unsalted butter, melted*
- *6 egg whites, beaten lightly*
- *Icing sugar, for dusting (optional)*

STAR ANISE SYRUP: *Juice of 3 oranges, strained*
- *4–6 whole star anise*
- *2/3 cup (150g/5oz) caster sugar*

Preheat oven to 210°C/425°F/Gas Mark 5.
Butter 10 friand tins, 1/2 cup (125ml/4fl oz)
capacity, or 12 muffin cups, 100ml (3fl oz) capacity.
Sift flour and icing sugar into a large bowl. Add
almond meal and rind; stir in butter and egg whites.
Beat with a wooden spoon until smooth. Spoon
mixture into prepared tins and bake for 15 minutes.
Reduce temperature to 200°C/400°F/Gas Mark 5
and bake for 10–15 minutes more, or until firm
to touch. Cool in tins for 5 minutes, turn out
and cool on a wire rack.

Combine syrup ingredients in a small saucepan
and heat, stirring, until sugar dissolves. Simmer for
5 minutes. Cool. Serve friands on plates with syrup
drizzled over, dusted with icing sugar, if desired.

Opposite: Orange Friands with Star Anise Syrup.

AFTERNOON TEA WHILE WATCHING TELEVISION

PANFORTE AND GLACÉ FRUIT

- *Rice paper*
- *125g (4oz) blanched almonds, roasted*
- *100g (3¹/₂oz) hazelnuts, roasted*
- *100g (3¹/₂oz) glacé apricots, cut into 6mm (¹/₄in) dice*
- *100g (3¹/₂oz) glacé peach, cut into 6mm (¹/₄in) dice*
- *100g (3¹/₂oz) citron, cut into 6mm (¹/₄in) dice*
- *²/₃ cup (100g/3¹/₂oz) plain flour*
- *2 tablespoons cocoa*
- *1 teaspoon cinnamon*
- *¹/₃ cup (75g/2¹/₂oz) raw sugar*
- *¹/₂ cup (125ml/4fl oz) honey*
- *125g (4oz) dark cooking chocolate, melted*
- *Icing sugar, for dusting*
- *Selection of glacé fruit*
  (oranges, plums, quinces), to serve

RICE PAPER

Rice paper is edible. It sticks to the base of the panforte and makes removal from the tin easy. Cut through it and serve panforte with paper attached.

Preheat oven to 160°C/325°F/Gas Mark 3. Line a deep 15 x 28cm (6 x 11in) baking tin with rice paper. Combine nuts and glacé fruit. Stir in sifted flour, cocoa and cinnamon. Combine raw sugar and honey in a deep saucepan and stir over medium heat until sugar dissolves. Boil for 5 minutes, or until toffee has reached the soft-ball stage (when a tiny amount forms a soft ball when dropped into a glass of cold water). Quickly add syrup and melted chocolate to nut mixture, stirring briskly to combine; immediately spread in prepared tin (be quick, the mixture rapidly becomes firm). Bake for 35 minutes. The panforte will be quite soft in the centre but hardens as it cools. If you leave it in the oven much longer the edges become very dry. Cool in tin, then wrap in foil and refrigerate for at least 1 day before cutting. (If wrapped and sealed, panforte will keep for several weeks in the refrigerator.) Dust thickly with icing sugar to serve with glacé fruit.

Opposite: Panforte and Glacé Fruit.

Mini pappadams are available from specialty food shops. Corn chips can be substituted.

HOT PARMESAN AND PESTO BITES

- *1 ¼ cups (100g/3 ½ oz) parmesan, freshly grated*
- *1 x 100g (3 ½ oz) jar fresh pesto*
- *2 sheets ready-rolled frozen puff pastry, thawed*

Preheat oven to 200°C/400°F/Gas Mark 5.
Line a baking tray with baking paper.
Mix 2 tablespoons parmesan into the pesto.
Spread remaining parmesan over work surface to cover an area the size of the pastry sheets.
Lay 1 sheet of pastry on parmesan and press down.
Spread top surface of pastry with half the pesto and fold both sides in to the centre. Repeat folding in twice to give a long roll. Do the same with the second pastry sheet.
With a sharp knife, cut rolls into slices 6mm (¼in) thick and place on baking tray, cut-sides-up-and-down. Cook for 8–10 minutes, or until golden and puffed. Serve hot.

AVOCADO MASH WITH CHILLI AND MINI PAPPADAMS

- *3 ripe avocados*
- *Juice of 2 limes*
- *1 teaspoon celery salt*
- *¼ cup (60ml/2 fl oz) sour cream*
- *1 tablespoon sweet chilli sauce*
- *Peanut oil, for shallow-frying*
- *300g (9 ½ oz) mini pappadams*

Mash all ingredients, except oil and pappadams, together to a fairly coarse texture. Spoon into a serving bowl.
Heat 5cm (2in) oil in a saucepan. It is hot enough when a pappadam dropped in immediately bubbles to the surface. Cook pappadams, in batches, for 10–15 seconds. Remove immediately with a wire scoop or slotted spoon and drain on paper towels. (The pappadams will continue to brown after removal from pan.) Serve with avocado mash.

Drinks at Twilight after the Matinée

Warm Custard Tarts

- 1 1/4 cups (190g/6oz) plain flour
- 250g (8oz) lard, at room temperature

Custard: 2/3 cup (150g/5oz) caster sugar
- 3 eggs
- 1/4 cup (60ml/2fl oz) milk

To make pastry, sift 1/2 cup (75g/2 1/2oz) of the flour into a basin. Cut lard into cubes and drop into flour; rub in with your fingers until combined to a solid paste. Scrape mixture onto baking paper, wrap and refrigerate until firm.

Sift remaining flour into a basin, add 1/3 cup (80ml/2 1/2 fl oz) cold water and mix to a firm dough. Turn out on a lightly floured work surface and knead until smooth. Roll into a rectangle 7.5 x 12cm (3 x 5in). Wrap rectangle in plastic wrap (film) and refrigerate for 20 minutes.

To make custard, combine sugar and 3/4 cup (190ml/6fl oz) water in a saucepan and stir over medium heat until sugar dissolves. Cool; beat lightly with eggs and milk.

On a heavily floured work surface, roll lard dough into a rectangle 15 x 12cm (6 x 5in).

CUSTARD TARTS

Buy custard tarts if you baulk at making the pastry, then warm in a low oven before serving.

Unwrap second rectangle, place on top of first and fold first over to enclose it completely. Turn the dough 90 degrees with the fold on your left side. Press dough lightly at intervals with the rolling pin. Roll out to a rectangle 12 x 30cm (5 x 12in). Fold both short ends in to meet at centre, then fold at centre so there are 4 layers. Repeat this roll and fold process 3 more times, with the fold always on your left side. Roll dough out to 3mm (1/8in) thickness.

Preheat oven to 220°C/450°F/Gas Mark 6. Lightly grease individual metal tart tins about 8.5cm (3 1/4in) in diameter.

Cut pastry to fit tart tins. Stand tins on a shallow oven tray and carefully pour in prepared custard (any drips between pastry and tin will make tart stick to tin). Bake for 8 minutes, reduce heat to 200°C/400°F/Gas Mark 5 and cook for 10 minutes, or until pastry is golden and custard is set. Stand in tins for 5 minutes; carefully lift out. Serve warm.

Makes 24.

BITES OF GLAZED CHICKEN BREAST ON CUCUMBER

- *1 cup (250ml/8fl oz) teriyaki sauce*
- *⅓ cup (90g/3oz) palm sugar, shaved or grated, or dark brown sugar*
- *3 green (spring) onions, chopped*
- *2 tablespoons sesame oil*
- *500g (1lb) skinless chicken breast fillet*
- *2—3 Lebanese cucumbers*

Purée teriyaki sauce, palm sugar, onions and 1 tablespoon sesame oil in a blender. Pour over chicken and marinate, covered and refrigerated, for at least 1 hour. Drain chicken, reserving marinade. Heat a non-stick frying pan, add remaining sesame oil and cook chicken over medium-high heat, turning and moving it around in pan frequently to prevent sugar in glaze from burning. Cut into 2.5cm (1in) dice.

Wash cucumber and cut into slices 6mm (¼in) thick. Place a cube of chicken on each, and arrange on a serving plate. Heat reserved marinade briefly and pour into a dipping container. Provide little wooden skewers and serve chicken at room temperature.

TOFU ROLLS WITH SALMON, WASABI AND VEGETABLE STICKS

- *2 sheets, 30cm (12in) square, dried tofu*
- *1 tablespoon wasabi paste*
- *200g (6½oz) fresh salmon*
- *2 carrots, thinly julienned*
- *2 sticks celery, thinly julienned*
- *½ daikon, thinly julienned*
- DIPPING SAUCE: *¼ cup (60ml/2fl oz) tamari, or light soy sauce*
- *¼ cup (60ml/2fl oz) ponzu sauce*

Rinse tofu sheets in cold water and lay out flat on a work surface. Spread half the wasabi thinly over each sheet. With a very sharp knife, slice salmon as thinly as you can. Spread over the wasabi. Along 1 edge of each tofu sheet, layer half the julienned vegetables. Roll up each tofu sheet, keeping the roll as tight as possible. (You will have 2 rolls about 4cm (1¾in) thick.) Wrap each tightly in plastic wrap (film) and refrigerate for at least 1 hour. Combine dipping sauce ingredients. To serve, remove plastic from rolls. With a very sharp knife, cut rolls into 4cm (1¾in) lengths. Arrange on a serving platter with dipping sauce in a small bowl.

JULIENNING
A mandolin is a compact, efficient, hand operated cutting device, with extremely sharp V-shaped blades, and attachments to allow for very thin or thick slicing, or thin or thick julienning. Firm vegetables and fruits are best cut with this tool.

DIPPING SAUCE
A simple alternative dipping sauce is fresh lime juice seasoned with sugar, salt and freshly ground black pepper to taste.

Opposite: Bites of Glazed Chicken Breast on Cucumber and Tofu Rolls with Salmon, Wasabi and Vegetable Sticks.

DINNER WITH GNOCCHI

SERVES SIX

Opposite: Gnocchi with Brussels Sprouts, Prosciutto and Parmesan.

BAKED RICOTTA

- *2 ¹/₂ cups (500g/1lb) fresh ricotta*
- *1 teaspoon olive oil*
- *1 teaspoon aniseed seeds*

Preheat oven to 160°C/325°F/Gas Mark 3.
Line a flat baking tray with baking paper. Press ricotta into a small sieve, levelling top. Drain for 10 minutes. Turn ricotta out directly on prepared tray. Try not to touch the surface and disturb the pattern left by the sieve. Sprinkle with oil and aniseed seeds. Bake for 40 minutes, or until turning golden. Cool to room temperature and serve with crackers and Lemon Chilli Pickle (recipe follows).

LEMON CHILLI PICKLE

- *8 thin-skinned lemons*
- *2 large red chillies, quartered*
- *2 teaspoons five-spice powder*
- *150g (5oz) palm sugar or dark brown sugar*

Place whole lemons in a pan of boiling water. Return to the boil for 5 minutes. Drain, cool until easy to handle; cut each into 8 segments, removing seeds and core membrane as you go. Combine in a deep saucepan with remaining ingredients. Bring to the boil, reduce heat to low and simmer, partly covered, for 30–40 minutes, or until thick and sticky. Spoon into sterilised jars, cool and seal (or use immediately, hot).
Makes about 3 cups.

GNOCCHI WITH BRUSSELS SPROUTS, PROSCIUTTO AND PARMESAN

- *500g (1lb) old floury potatoes, washed*
- *1 ⅓ cups (200g/6½oz) plain flour*
- *60g (2oz) butter*
- *24 brussels sprouts*
- *24 very thin slices prosciutto*
- *Shaved parmesan, to serve*

Place whole unpeeled potatoes in a large saucepan,
cover with cold water and bring to the boil. Reduce
heat and simmer for 20–25 minutes, or until
potatoes are cooked through. (If skins start to split,
you have cooked them too long.) Remove immediately.
Drain and cool until easy to handle; peel. While still
warm, push potatoes through a ricer onto a work
surface. Sift flour onto potatoes and knead together
until combined. Handle as lightly as possible. The
mixture should be soft and firm. If sticky, add a little
more flour. Cut into pieces the size of tennis balls
and roll each on a lightly floured surface into a snake
about 2cm (¾in) in diameter. Cut each snake
into 2.5cm (1in) lengths.
Line a large flat tray or baking trays with baking paper
and dust lightly with flour. Take 1 piece of dough and
quickly roll between your palms to a neat oval shape.
Dip a fork in flour. With your thumb, gently press
this rolled piece onto back of a fork so the tines make
ridges on the underside, and your thumbs a concave
indent in top. Flick gnocchi off onto the tray.

Repeat with remaining mixture, keeping gnocchi in
a single layer on tray(s). The gnocchi are best used
the same day, but can, at this stage, be covered and
frozen; cook frozen, do not thaw.
Melt butter in an ovenproof serving dish and keep
warm in a 150°C/300°F/Gas Mark 2 oven. To cook
brussels sprouts, trim stem ends, remove any
blemished outside leaves and cut sprouts into
quarters. Drop into a large pot of boiling water and
cook for 8–10 minutes. Remove with a slotted spoon
to the serving dish, toss in butter and keep warm.
Put half the gnocchi (do not crowd pan) into same
boiling water and cook until they rise to the surface.
Flip over, cook for 30 seconds more and remove with
a slotted spoon to the serving dish. Turn with
a rubber spatula to mix with butter and brussels
sprouts. Repeat with remaining gnocchi.
Place prosciutto in a single layer in a large frying pan
or under a preheated grill and cook until fairly crisp.
Serve gnocchi and brussels sprouts in warmed bowls,
with prosciutto crumbled over. Top with parmesan
and freshly ground black pepper.

TAMARILLOS POACHED WITH SLICED TANGELO

- *1 cup (200g (6½oz) brown sugar*
- *1 vanilla pod, split lengthways*
- *12 tamarillos*
- *2 tangelos, washed (or Honey Murcott mandarins)*
- *Thick cream or ice-cream, to serve*

Place sugar and 4 cups (1L/32fl oz) water and
vanilla pod in a deep frying pan. Heat until
simmering and sugar is dissolved.
With a small, sharp knife, make a shallow cross on
tip of each tamarillo. Slice tangelos as thinly as
possible, removing seeds. Place fruit and any juice
in simmering syrup, cover and cook on lowest heat,
turning occasionally for 15–20 minutes.
Turn off heat and cool fruit in syrup. To serve, remove
tamarillos with a slotted spoon, peel (leaving stalks
intact) and arrange on serving plates. Boil syrup and
tangelos to reduce syrup by about half; spoon over
fruit. Serve with thick cream or ice-cream.

DINNER WITH HOMEMADE PASTA

| SERVES SIX

PROVOLONE

Provolone piccante is a cow milk cheese from southern
Italy. It has a firm texture and mild, smoky flavour.

BAKED ROLLS OF EGGPLANT,
OLIVE PASTE AND PROVOLONE

- *1 large eggplant (aubergine)*
- *100g (3¹/₂oz) black olive paste*
- *250g (8oz) provolone piccante*
- *Olive oil*

Preheat oven to 200°C/400°F/Gas Mark 5.
Cut eggplant in 12 thin slices from stem to base.
Spread 1 side of each with olive paste and shaved
provolone. Roll each slice, starting from stem end,
and secure with a toothpick. Place in a single layer
in a shallow, lightly oiled ovenproof dish and drizzle
with olive oil. Bake for 20 minutes, reducing
temperature to 190°C/375°F/Gas Mark 4 after
15 minutes if rolls are becoming too browned.
Pass around hot or at room temperature,
as a casual entrée. Provide napkins.

PAPPARDELLE WITH BAKED BEETROOT, RADICCHIO AND TUNA

- *6 beetroot*
- *4 cups (625g/1¼lb) unbleached bread flour*
- *4 eggs*
- *90g (3oz) butter*
- *600g (1¼lb) fresh tuna*
- *1 small head radicchio*
- *Juice and rind of 1 lemon*
- *⅓ cup (80ml/2½fl oz) balsamic vinegar*

Preheat oven to 180°C/350°F/Gas Mark 4.
Line baking dish with aluminium foil. Trim beetroot leaves, leaving about 1cm (½in) of stems. Place beetroot in baking dish, cover with foil and bake for 1 hour. Cool until easy to handle, then slip skins off and discard.

To make pappardelle, place flour in a mound on a work surface, make a well in centre and break in eggs. Using a long metal spatula, break up eggs and slowly incorporate flour, working in from the outer edge. (You may need to add either more flour or a few drops of water to get a smooth dough.) Knead with your hands into a ball, then flatten. Break dough into 4 pieces and pass each through a pasta machine, rolling and folding 10 times on the widest setting, then once through each of the remaining settings.

Hang over a (clean) broom handle suspended between 2 chairs or in another suitable place, to dry slightly before cutting. (Another idea is to place a tea towel over an open cupboard door and drape pasta over this.)

To cut, fold each sheet into a roll 10cm (4in) wide, and using a sharp knife, cut pasta into ribbons 2.5cm (1in) wide. Unfold and pile pasta on a tray.

Heat a large pot of water to boiling, drop in pasta and cook for 5 minutes, stirring occasionally. Turn off heat, stand in water for 1 minute, drain and serve. To cook tuna, heat half the butter with freshly ground black pepper to taste in a frying pan. Add tuna and cook over high heat for 1 minute on each side (this seals and browns tuna, but inside remains rare). Remove from pan.

Cut radicchio in half, then into thin wedges. Cut each beetroot into eighths. Melt remaining butter in pan; add lemon juice and rind and balsamic vinegar. Add beetroot and radicchio and cook, stirring, over gentle heat to warm beetroot and just wilt radicchio. Slice tuna thinly. Serve pappardelle in bowls with tuna and beetroot mixture spooned over.

GLAZED LATE FIGS WITH BROWN-SUGAR ZABAGLIONE

- *500g (1lb) late-harvest green figs*
  (these are tiny, with firm skins and intensely pink flesh)
- *½ cup (100g/3½oz) brown sugar*
  ZABAGLIONE: *5 egg yolks*
- *⅓ cup (75g/2½oz) brown sugar*
- *½ cup (125ml/4fl oz) brandy*

Wash figs and place in a heavy-based saucepan with sugar and ¼ cup (60ml/2fl oz) water. Cover and cook over medium heat, stirring occasionally, for 20 minutes. Remove lid, reduce heat to low and cook for 20 minutes more. Figs will remain whole and become glazed. The syrup will be dark and almost like toffee. Serve immediately, or transfer to a covered container and refrigerate until required.

Bring to room temperature to serve.
To make zabaglione, whisk yolks and brown sugar in the top of a double boiler, or a bowl placed over a saucepan of simmering water, until smooth and thick. Slowly whisk in brandy, stirring over medium heat until sauce thickens and is well aerated.

Serve warm.

Opposite: Pappardelle with Baked Beetroot, Radicchio and Tuna.

SUPPER FOR CARDS OR BACKGAMMON

JERUSALEM ARTICHOKE SOUP WITH HORSERADISH QUENELLES

HORSERADISH QUENELLES: *2 egg yolks*
- *1 tablespoon butter, melted*
- *¼ cup (60ml/2 fl oz) creamed cottage cheese*
- *1 tablespoon horseradish sauce*
- *¼ cup (15g/½oz) fresh white breadcrumbs*
- *Finely grated rind of ½ lemon*
- *¼ cup chopped chives*

JERUSALEM ARTICHOKE SOUP:
- *500g (1lb) Jerusalem artichokes, scrubbed*
- *¼ cup (60ml/2 fl oz) lemon juice*
- *1 teaspoon sea salt*
- *1 ¼ cups (300ml/10 fl oz) pouring cream*
- *1 tablespoon butter*
- *4 medium tomatoes, peeled and chopped*
- *1 clove garlic*
- *Italian (flat-leaf) parsley, to garnish*

ARTICHOKES
Jerusalem artichokes are tubers from a plant similar to the sunflower. They are not to be confused with globe artichokes. Jerusalem artichokes are sometimes also called sun chokes.

To make quenelles, whisk egg yolks with butter until frothy; stir in remaining ingredients. Cover and stand at room temperature while making soup.

Slice artichokes thickly; combine in a deep saucepan with lemon juice, salt and enough cold water just to cover. Bring to the boil and simmer, partly covered, for 15–20 minutes, or until tender. Drain and cool slightly, then purée with cream.

Meanwhile, melt butter in clean saucepan, add tomato and garlic and cook gently until tomato has broken up. Purée with artichoke, pour back into saucepan and warm over low heat (do not boil).

To cook quenelles, heat 5cm (2in) water until barely simmering in a deep frying pan. Using 2 tablespoons, shape quenelle mixture into oval dumplings and carefully lower each into the simmering water; cook for about 10 minutes. Regulate temperature so water remains at a simmer (boiling will break up quenelles). Serve soup in warmed jumbo cups or soup bowls. Remove cooked quenelles with a slotted spoon and place on top of soup. Garnish with Italian (flat-leaf) parsley.

Opposite: Jerusalem Artichoke Soup with Horseradish Quenelles.

FLOURLESS CHOCOLATE LIQUEUR CAKE

- $1/2$ cup $(75g/2\,1/2\,oz)$ hazelnuts
- $125g$ $(4oz)$ unsalted butter
- $110g$ $(3\,1/2\,oz)$ dark cooking chocolate
- 3 tablespoons Drambuie
- 2 tablespoons pure cocoa powder
- 2 eggs
- $1/3$ cup $(75g/2\,1/2\,oz)$ brown sugar
- 1 teaspoon vanilla

FROSTING:

- $110g$ $(3\,1/2\,oz)$ dark cooking chocolate
- 1 tablespoon Drambuie
- 1 tablespoon light corn syrup
- *Thick cream and fresh berries, to serve*

Preheat oven to 180°C/350°F/Gas Mark 4.
Lightly butter a 15cm (6in) square cake tin.
Line base with baking paper.

Roast hazelnuts in oven for 8–10 minutes. Cool,
then grind to a fine meal. Melt butter and chocolate in
a bowl over simmering water or in a microwave oven.
Cool slightly; stir in Drambuie, hazelnuts and cocoa.

Beat egg with sugar in an electric mixer on high
speed for about 5 minutes, or until thick. Fold into
chocolate mixture and pour into prepared tin.

Bake for 35–40 minutes, or until top feels firm
to a gentle touch, but a skewer inserted in centre
comes out slightly sticky. Cool in tin on a wire rack
for 5 minutes; loosen sides with a small metal spatula.
Cool completely in tin. Turn out onto a flat plate.
For frosting, melt remaining chocolate, add Drambuie
and beat in vanilla and corn syrup until mixture is
smooth and glossy. Cool until beginning to thicken;
spread over cake. Leave to firmly set. Serve small
slices of cake with cream and fresh berries (raspberries
or mulberries are a delicious foil to this rich cake).

SUPPER AND COGNAC BY THE FIRE

| SERVES FOUR TO SIX

DUCK PÂTÉ AND CRACKERS

- 2 bunches fresh sage
- 2 whole duck breasts, on bone
- 2 tablespoons mustard seed oil
- 30g (1oz) butter
- 1 tablespoon mustard seeds
- 2 medium onions, chopped
- ½ cup (125ml/4fl oz) cream
- 2 small leaves gelatine

Spread 1 bunch of sage in base of a steamer pot and place duck, bone-side-down, on top. Steam over simmering water for 25–30 minutes, or until duck is thoroughly cooked. Cool.

Heat oil and butter in a frying pan, add mustard seeds and onion and cook, stirring, until onion is translucent.

Cut duck meat off bone and process to a smooth paste with onion mixture and cream in a food processor or blender. Spoon into a small serving bowl, cover and refrigerate until firm.

Place remaining sage in a small jug, pour on ½ cup (125ml/4fl oz) boiling water and stand for 15 minutes. Soak gelatine in cold water until soft. Squeeze out excess water and place gelatine in a small saucepan. Strain sage liquid into saucepan and reheat, stirring until gelatine dissolves. Pour over surface of cold pâté, and leave until set. Serve with a selection of crackers and breads.

ABOUT PASTRY
Frozen ready-rolled pastry is a very useful stand-by. Separate sheets of ready-rolled puff pastry, while still frozen, by slipping a long spatula between them. Leave on plastic to thaw.

LITTLE MUSHROOM AND LEEK TARTS

- 2 sheets ready-rolled frozen puff pastry, thawed
- 30g (1oz) butter
- 1 leek, white part only, finely chopped
- 2 cloves garlic, chopped
- 1 teaspoon fennel seeds
- 200g (6½ oz) shiitake mushrooms, finely sliced
- ½ cup (125ml/4fl oz) sour cream
- 1 egg, beaten lightly

Using an 7.5cm (3in) fluted cookie cutter, cut rounds from pastry and place in lightly oiled 100ml (3fl oz) muffin tins. Refrigerate.

Preheat oven to 200°C/400°F/Gas Mark 5. Melt butter in a frying pan and cook leek, garlic and fennel seeds, stirring occasionally, until leek is soft. Add mushrooms and stir over medium heat for 5 minutes. Cool slightly. Stir in combined sour cream and egg and season to taste with salt and black pepper. Spoon mixture into pastry cases and bake for 20 minutes, or until pastry is golden and puffed. Serve hot.

Makes 18.

CHESTNUT AND BRANDY TRUFFLES

- *250g (8oz) dark cooking chocolate*
- *250g (8oz) can sweetened chestnut purée with vanilla*
- *2 tablespoons brandy*
- *Pure cocoa powder, for coatng truffles*

Melt chocolate in a bowl over simmering water or in a microwave oven. (Do not let steam contact chocolate.) Remove from heat. Add chestnut purée and brandy, stirring until smooth. Refrigerate until cold and firm enough to roll. Sift cocoa powder onto a shallow plate. Roll truffle mixture into walnut-size balls, roll in cocoa and place on a tray lined with baking paper. Store between layers of baking paper in an airtight container in the refrigerator until required.

RUM TRUFFLES

- *250g (8oz) dark cooking chocolate*
- *1 cup (200ml/6½fl oz) crème fraîche*
- *2 tablespoons dark rum, Grand Marnier or brandy*
- *Pure cocoa powder, for coating truffles*

Melt chocolate in a bowl over simmering water or in a microwave oven. (Do not let steam contact chocolate.) Remove from heat. Warm crème fraîche in a small saucepan until just starting to simmer at edges. Stir into chocolate until smooth. Stir in rum. Refrigerate until cold and firm enough to roll. Sift cocoa powder onto a shallow plate. Roll truffle mixture into walnut-size balls, roll in cocoa and place on a tray lined with baking paper. Store between layers of baking paper in an airtight container in the refrigerator until required.

CHOCOLATE TRUFFLES

The rum mixture is softer than the chestnut mixture—be prepared to get sticky hands. Alternatively roll truffles in roasted or chopped nuts, toasted desiccated coconut, or finely chopped glacé fruit, or dip in melted chocolate. Brandy-marinated prunes can be chopped and stirred through truffle mixture. Refrigerate and roll as recipe instructs.

Opposite: Rum Truffles and Chestnut and Brandy Truffles.

MEASUREMENTS

In New Zealand, South Africa, Canada, USA and England, 1 tablespoon equals 15ml. In Australia, 1 tablespoon equals 20ml. These variations will not affect the end result, as long as the same spoon is used. The difference between measuring cups internationally is within 2 or 3 teaspoons. One Australian metric cup holds 250ml.

INDEX